Economy
and
the Future

Studies in Violence, Mimesis, and Culture

Economy and the Future

A CRISIS OF FAITH

Jean-Pierre Dupuy

Translated by M. B. DeBevoise

Michigan State University Press · *East Lansing*

♾ The paper used in this publication meets the minimum requirements of ANSI/NISO Z39.48-1992 (R 1997) (Permanence of Paper).

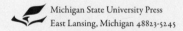 Michigan State University Press
East Lansing, Michigan 48823-5245

Printed and bound in the United States of America.

20 19 18 17 16 15 14   1 2 3 4 5 6 7 8 9 10

LIBRARY OF CONGRESS CONTROL NUMBER: 2014936109
ISBN: 978-1-61186-146-4 (pbk.)
ISBN: 978-1-60917-433-0 (ebook: PDF)
ISBN: 978-1-62895-033-5 (ebook: ePub)
ISBN: 978-1-62896-032-7 (ebook: Mobi/prc)

Book design and composition by Charlie Sharp, Sharp Des!gns, Lansing, Michigan
Cover design by David Drummond, Salamander Design, www.salamanderhill.com
Cover image is *Bull* (oil on canvas) by Cacouault, Daniel (Contemporary Artist)/Private Collection/The Bridgeman Art Library. Used with permission.

g green press INITIATIVE Michigan State University Press is a member of the Green Press Initiative and is committed to developing and encouraging ecologically responsible publishing practices. For more information about the Green Press Initiative and the use of recycled paper in book publishing, please visit *www.greenpressinitiative.org*.

Visit Michigan State University Press at *www.msupress.org*

Time is the substance of which I am made.
Time is a river that carries me away, but I am the river;
it is a tiger that tears me apart, but I am the tiger;
it is a fire that consumes me, but I am the fire.

—Jorge Luis Borges, "A New Refutation of Time"

Contents

The Bewilderment of Politics

A sense of shame led me to write this book. Shame at seeing politics allow itself to be humiliated by economics, at seeing political authority disgraced by managerialism, by the cult of business management.

Authority, managerialism—these are abstractions. A somewhat ridiculous allegorical image comes to mind: the sovereign people, pictured in the same manner as the multitude of citizens that fills out the body of Leviathan in the frontispiece to the first edition of Hobbes's famous work of that name, only now the giant figure has lost his crown and bows his head before the chief executive officer of the realm. At least a part of this image—the giant's head, the political class, composed of the men and women who have chosen to serve the state—is not allegorical, however.[1] There is something pathetic about seeing high officials reduced to a state of abject obeisance, as we do today, government ministers prepared to make any compromise, ready to show any weakness for fear of frightening or annoying the exalted person before whom they cower. But is it a person at all? No. It, too, is a pure abstraction. And it, too, curiously, is a multitude, since we use the plural in speaking of it. We refer to the "markets," just as in the Bible the word *Elohim*, a masculine plural noun in Hebrew, meaning the gods, is used to speak of *the* one God: "In the beginning, God [*Elohim*] created the heavens and the earth" (Genesis 1:1).[2] What could this plural form, the "markets," really signify, if not the manifold and intertwining tentacles of a great monster, sluggish, craven, and dumb, which takes fright at the slightest noise—and in this way brings about the very thing that it shrinks from in terror: turbulence in the global markets?

Setting aside this rather fantastic image, what are we left with? Men and women in positions of power who, by prostrating themselves before a phantasm, transform it into something real and, at the same time, endow it with extraordinary power. For the market (as the "markets" are often called, by way of shorthand) resembles another monster, the one that roams a distant planet colonized by human scientists in Fred M. Wilcox's cinematic masterpiece of science fiction, a projection of Dr. Morbius's own subconscious.[3] This today is the lot of politics: to battle against an army of nightmarish shadows—not in a dream, but in the real world.

"The future head of the Italian government, Mario Monti, appealed to the markets yesterday for a bit of time in order to form a cabinet and to implement an austerity program. He announced that Italians might have to make 'sacrifices' once he had taken the oath of office and put his program into effect. His appointment was welcomed by the markets, but anxiety persisted and soon regained the upper hand."[4] The particular case hardly matters; in an age when all values have been turned upside down, one reads or hears the like of this almost every day.[5] Except for a small minority of vocal protesters, whose numbers may nevertheless be growing, no one is bothered in the least by this way of talking anymore. "Mr. Executioner, one moment, please."[6] Thus the plea of every head of state called upon to rescue his country from economic ruin, hoping to stay a bit longer the fall of the blade of the financial guillotine, and with it the sentencing of whole populations to a bleak future whose flickering beacons are rising unemployment and shrinking access to education and other basic social services. The new master of whichever country finds itself in dire financial straits this month—they come one after the other, in a sequence announced by the markets through their spokesmen, the international agencies charged with monitoring global economic stability—officiates like a high priest. As a rule, he knows Olympus and its gods well enough to have served already in one of their main temples. A practiced maker of sacrifices, he prepares to offer up to the gods, in a holocaust, the number of victims they have demanded. Is there anyone who does not see that these infamous terms are borrowed from the most primitive conception of the sacred, and constitute an incomprehensible retreat from the most fundamental values of modern democracy?

But the capitulation of politics to economics is still more contemptible than this. When a ruling party warns that the markets would countermand the will of the people if the opposition were to come to power and punish the country by plunging it into catastrophe; when a country sure of its economic superiority uses the pressure exerted by the markets to make an example of its neighbors, disciplining them like so many naughty schoolchildren; when the prospect of a referendum in the country where democracy was invented raises the specter of popular revolt there, and throws governments elsewhere in Europe into a panic—in every case it is the political class that kneels before the titans of finance and makes itself their lackey. Every time the political class avows its determination to take on the markets and congratulates itself for having avoided the worst, at least for the moment, authority places itself on the same level as managerialism: whether it wins or loses does not matter, for it has already debased itself, and will go on debasing itself, by virtue of its very willingness to fight, like a teacher who lowers himself to trade blows with unruly students.

And the role of economists in all of this? It would do them a great honor if we were to credit them with responsibility for the absolute triumph of their profession. It is their job to chart the course of economic activity and to explain how the economy works; naturally, then, we look to them to help us make sense of what, on the face of it, is a senseless state of affairs. And yet they are the first ones to demonstrate that they understand nothing. This has not prevented them, however, from showing still greater arrogance, as though they alone were qualified to think about what they are pleased to call "the crisis"; as though they alone, humbly assisted by politicians having only a very approximate mastery of the basic concepts of economic theory, were able to find a way out from this crisis—whereas it is their own blindness to social reality that is responsible for a large share of the world's troubles.

The shame I felt was intensified on learning that two American economists who had recently been awarded the Nobel Prize took the opportunity provided by this honor to lecture Europeans. One of them made a point of insisting that "there are no new questions *for economic theory* regarding

Europe and the euro." Well, then, one might ask, if the solution to the problem is known, why has it not been put into effect? "Resolving the sovereign debt crisis in the eurozone is child's play," answered the other laureate. "From an economic point of view at least. The stumbling block is politics."[7]

I beg to differ: the stumbling block—the *skandálon,* as the inventors of democracy would have said—is economics; or, as we might more aptly say, following Hobbes in his name for the absolute sovereign, Economy. Here I am not thinking especially of financial capitalism, or even of capitalism in the broadest sense. Nor am I thinking of speculative markets, whether regulated or unregulated, bullish or bearish. No, what I have in mind is the place that economic affairs, as well as the professional study of these affairs, occupy both in our personal lives and in the functioning of the societies in which we live. The role Economy plays is exorbitant by any reasonable standard—and yet we find nothing in the least unusual about this. Not only has the influence of Economy spread throughout the world, it has taken over our very ways of thinking about the world. Plainly, then, it is not the analysis of economic behavior, which we call economics, that will reveal to us the meaning of this massive and extraordinary phenomenon, for in that case it would preside as judge and jury at its own trial.[8] Only from a more remote perspective, freed from the sway of Economy, will it be possible to find a reason for astonishment at what now is taken for granted by the modern citizen, who has wholly and completely become, without even knowing it, *Homo economicus.*

But why should anyone be troubled by the fact that economics has made politics its servant? Historically, it is often the case that one domain of human activity supplants another. Politics itself found it necessary to assert its independence from religion, while at the same time assigning it a subordinate status in the name of social unity and the defense of the state. Why should economics not now assume ascendancy, mobilizing the virtues of competence and efficiency in support of the general welfare, while politics is left to serve as a harmless outlet for the clash of irrational passions?

The present work is intended as a reply to this very objection. I maintain that such a transfer of supremacy, unopposed by any obstacle, would spell the end not only of economics and politics, but of civilization itself. Modern societies, in pulling down all the old barriers, all the prohibitions, rituals, and symbolic conceptions that once worked to curb human violence, unleashed new forces of unprecedented creativity. But these were counterbalanced by new forces of unprecedented destructiveness, so that the world was transformed into a single community of human beings living under the threat of being reduced to ashes, scattered among piles of radioactive rubble.

Little by little, Economy emancipated itself from the shackles of the sacred. Once held in check by religion, and then by politics, it has today become both our religion *and* our politics. No longer subject to any higher authority, it cannot decide our future, or make us a world in which to live: it has become our future *and* our world. Advanced postindustrial societies have been well and truly mystified, in the original sense of that word, and their politicians hoodwinked. The result is paralysis.

◆　◆　◆

In thinking about how best to develop these ideas I considered several styles of exposition, and finally settled upon a genre that I may perhaps claim to have invented myself: the metaphysical broadside. I chose it in preference to others because it seemed to me necessary to use all available means, not excluding derision and mockery, to combat the extraordinary assault on humanity we are presently witnessing. But it is intended as something more than a mere lampoon. In its aims and purposes it is primarily philosophical, because I am convinced that the malignant dominion exerted by Economy today instills a poison, drop by drop, that penetrates to the very depths of our being and infects our most fundamental categories of thought. If civilization can yet be saved from extinction, the change in attitude this requires of us must be, first and foremost, metaphysical in nature.

I have chosen furthermore to develop my argument with reference to the metaphysics of time. Not only has Economy invented a new conception of the future, it has given it unprecedented scope. This is part of what is meant by the original title of my book in French, *L'avenir de l'économie*: the relationship to the future that Economy makes possible, but only so long as it relies on the visionary powers of politics. When politics is preeminent, rather than subordinate, so that economics is properly understood to mean political economy, the effect is to open the future up to us, rather than to close it off. It is precisely that positive relationship to time, in the absence of which we are powerless to look forward in our lives with confidence and resolve, which now stands in danger of being forever lost. This is the other part of what is meant by the book's title, its ordinary sense, having to do with the future of the economy and, more generally, of economic life. The menace that hangs over the world today is that economic life as we know it may have no future. Economy now finds itself haunted by the dread of its own demise.

I lay out the argument in four parts:

1. The desacralization of the world that is the outstanding characteristic, perhaps even the destiny, of the modern age, and the rationalist outlook that is both its cause and its consequence, gave birth to a new regime of evil. I begin by showing that Economy, the companion of this new regime, came forward to fill the place left vacant by the retreat from the sacred. Like the sacred before it, Economy *contains* violence in the two senses of that term: it erects a barrier against violence by violent means. It is this mechanism of self-exteriorization that allows "good" violence to overcome "bad" violence, and permits us in turn to understand why Montesquieu and other thinkers placed such faith in commerce—the only thing, they believed, that was capable of putting an end to the gruesome wars of religion that consumed Europe during the early modern period. In our own time, only the one-eyed and the blinkered, who see the vices of the capitalist system and nothing else, could rejoice in the prospect of its dissolution without pausing to ask themselves what will fill the void. For today we are aware that bad and good violence are, in the last analysis, the same violence. This lucidity has a price, however, for it utterly undermines the foundations of the present economic order, and we are at a loss to say what should be put in its place.

2. The peculiar logic of exteriorization I have just described, in which violence places itself outside itself, so to speak, has traditionally been referred to by philosophers as "self-transcendence." I go on in the second part to show that this logic, not the purely internal state that economists call "equilibrium," is what underlies the self-organizing properties of markets. The self-transcendence of market prices provides a first example. Even here one cannot help noticing the inadequacy of the metaphysical foundations of neoclassical economic theory. I am chiefly concerned, however, with the way in which the mechanism of self-transcendence operates to create a future in the minds of economic agents. An economy functions by projecting itself into a future that does not yet exist, but that it brings into existence by allowing itself to be pulled forward in time, as it were, until it reaches the very moment when

the future it has imagined becomes real. This conundrum belongs to the category of so-called bootstrapping paradoxes, of which the imaginary exploits of Baron Münchausen supply a pleasing and striking instance.

One case is of particular interest in this connection, in which all agents coordinate their behavior with reference to the same self-transcendent image of the future. Its interest derives from a set of remarkable properties that make it possible to resolve an otherwise intractable problem (assuming one refrains from invoking a deus ex machina, in this case ethics), namely, of accounting for the existence of such evanescent notions as trust and confidence in the open-endedness of the future, without which capitalism could not function. It is owing to these things, in other words, that Economy becomes moral and political. This does not mean that it takes the place of politics, quite to the contrary. Without politics, without access to a domain that is separate from it, even transcendent, economic life is incapable of flourishing. It is exactly the capacity of politics to go beyond itself, to transcend itself, that furnishes an economy with the resources that are vital to its survival, that keep it from dying. In a world where everything has a price, however, where economics can be said to buy politics—in the sense not only that it corrupts politics, but also that it drags politics down to its own level, since elected officials can now simply be paid off—politics is deprived of its power of self-transcendence. In this world economics dooms itself to extinction at the same moment that it condemns politics to the same fate.

3. I go on in the third part to advance a bold conjecture, but one that is firmly grounded in both theory and fact. The extraordinary irrationality of markets, the sheer madness revealed by the formation of bubbles on an international scale and by the devastating crashes that inevitably follow them, arises from a deep-seated, and no doubt quite unconscious, sense of impending catastrophe shared by the executive officers of global capitalism. These immensely powerful people, in their heart of hearts, no longer believe in the future. This, I suspect, is the mainspring of the present crisis: the mechanisms of self-transcendence are jammed, perhaps irreversibly, with the result that Economy is quickly losing its capacity to act as a barrier against violence. The end of economic history, at least in its capitalist phase, is an extreme illustration of catastrophes whose occurrence is certain but whose date is unknown. On a personal level, all of us have to come to terms with the fact that, sooner

or later, we will die. And yet today no aspect of human existence, not even the ending of it, is immune to the hegemonic pretensions of neoclassical economic thought. Not only the intellectual poverty, but also the emotional poverty, of what it has to say about death give us little reason to believe that it will be able to face up to the fact of its own mortality.

4. I come back in the fourth part to the metaphysical problem of coordinating individual behaviors by means of the future. This leads me to consider two paradoxes that have yet to be satisfactorily resolved: one a paradox of historical and religious anthropology associated with Max Weber, having to do with the curious affinity between the emergence of the capitalist spirit and the Calvinist doctrine of predestination, at least in the interpretation given to it by the Puritan settlers of New England; the other, a logical and metaphysical paradox due, it is said, to the physicist William Newcomb. Having first shown that these two paradoxes are in fact identical, I then propose a novel solution. In the light of this solution, the conditions needing to be satisfied if mere economics is ever to be able to go beyond itself and become a genuinely political and moral economy appear to be at once altogether unreasonable and eminently sensible: unreasonable, because they lead us to reject the very axioms that economists cherish most of all, axioms that provide the basis of what they are accustomed to think of as rational behavior; sensible, because every one of us violates these axioms in making the most important decisions of our lives. Indeed, if we did not violate them, we would not be social creatures. In this sense, strangely enough, we are all Calvinist Puritans.

I then proceed to show, finally, that satisfying these same metaphysical conditions also makes it possible for a democratic community of citizens to be transformed into its opposite, a society of isolated individuals, each of whom has taken refuge in a private world of consumption. Here we see the ambivalence of Economy with regard to the problem of evil. Everything depends on faith—the faith of the Calvinists, in this case, perverted by the bad faith of individual economic agents, whom neoclassical theory has elevated to the status of "sovereign" consumers. In a consumer society we are all *strangers* to each other, in the sense that Camus gave this term: we believe, and yet at the same time do not believe, that we can live independently of others, for we desperately need them to be convinced that we do not need them. The individualism of economic man (or woman) can therefore be seen for what it is, a sham, an immensely elaborate hoax that society plays on itself.

The brief chapter with which I conclude the book will come as a surprise to those who think they understand what I mean when I speak of humanity's catastrophic future—an idea that has shaped my thinking and guided my writing over the past ten years, and that has caused me to be accused of "fatalism." The solution I propose to the paradox associated with Newcomb and, more famously, Weber makes it possible to show that the true fatalists are not the enlightened doomsayers whom I have called upon to come forward and make their voices heard, but rather all those who have been taken in by a counterfeit and dishonest sort of individualism, all those who, having been made fools of by Economy, confuse the freedom praised by Milton Friedman[9] with its supermarket version—the freedom to choose between thirty brands of detergent.

◆　◆　◆

Is it possible to think intelligently about Economy without being a professional economist? Not only is it possible, it is an urgent necessity. For if economic thought remains the monopoly of economists, it will go on being mired in feeble-mindedness. Yet simply to pose the questions I discuss in this book, to say nothing of the manner in which I try to answer them, is evidently disqualifying. Anyone who claims, as I do, that unless these questions are honestly faced up to the "science" economists proudly imagine themselves to practice, trapped in an autistic void of their own devising, will remain impotent to explain actual economic behavior—anyone who claims such a thing is bound to be drummed out of the profession.

It is true that a growing minority of economists is now prepared to admit that orthodox economic theory has failed. Their candor is as praiseworthy as it is welcome. And yet when they try to say how and why it has failed, there is nothing but noise.[10] I maintain, heretically, that only by freeing ourselves from the hold of economic theory, in breaking the spell it has over us, will it be possible to understand the nature of the sickness from which it suffers. This does not mean, as some dissident economists suppose, that refuge can be had in one or more of the other social sciences, whether sociology, or anthropology, or political science, or game theory, or cognitive science, or some combination of these. Surely it is too late for that. To one degree or another these disciplines have already been bewildered by Economy themselves. Economic theory continues to enjoy unrivaled prestige, owing to the rigor of its mathematical formalization and the aura of the Nobel Prize. But so long as its philosophical foundations remain unstated, and unjustified, we are left with a series of choices that are unfortunate to exactly the extent they are unreflective. If they have not been properly thought through, this is because they have seemed to go without saying. They have seemed, in other words, perfectly logical.

The lexicon of French is considerably poorer than that of English. But sometimes this works to its advantage. The word *l'économie* is a fine example. It may be used to refer to a domain, or dimension, of social reality—what in English is called "the economy"—or to a point of view, or vantage point, on the whole of that reality—what in English is called "economics." The coincidence of these two senses in French brings out a tacit connection between the domain and the point of view. Note, however, that this is not the same connection that an object shares with its mirror image, for the discipline of economics has proved to be mistaken about the reality it studies; nor are we dealing here with a discipline that is capable of remaking reality in its own image, for whereas economic theories, whether they are true or false, have an undoubted impact on reality, reality nonetheless retains its causal independence. The bond uniting economic theory and social life therefore cannot be characterized in either realist or idealist terms. It is a complex phenomenon, one that a long line of anthropologists in the French tradition, from Marcel Mauss to Pierre Bourdieu, has described as a kind of social hypocrisy—*un mensonge collectif à soi-même*; literally, a collective lying to oneself.

It is here that we encounter a puzzle. There is a work, by a noneconomist as it happens, that anyone who claims to be familiar with the circumstances surrounding the birth of modern economic theory cannot have failed to read, whose pivotal chapter, on which the whole argument turns, bears almost exactly the same title in its French translation: "Sur le mensonge à soi-même." In this chapter the author demonstrates that what we now call economic behavior is not at all economic in the ordinary sense of the term. Then, as now, if people ceaselessly hunger after material wealth, it is not because what they seek to obtain by means of wealth is the satisfaction of material needs, which after all could be met with a finite quantity of resources. To the contrary, the unlimited nature of our appetite is an unmistakable sign that its

Introduction   xix

object is immaterial and infinite: one always wants more. Economic theory is fond of pretending that it is concerned with the rational use of scarce resources. Appealing to etymology, it regards economics as the study of the *nomos* of the *oikos*, which is to say the laws or conventions governing the management of household affairs. The author of whom I speak takes issue with this characterization in the strongest possible terms. An economy, he says, is governed by desire—and, more particularly, by the individual's desire to be admired by others. Of this kind of admiration, colored as it is by envy, it is never possible to have enough.

Nevertheless, our author goes on to say, an economy can function only so long as individuals are ignorant of their own motivations, no less than the motivations of others. They believe, wrongly, that wealth will bring them the material well-being that they believe, wrongly as well, to be necessary to their happiness. Even though they are mistaken in attributing to wealth virtues it does not have, by coveting it they end up being right after all. For wealth, as it turns out, does indeed have the virtues it is believed to have—but only *because* it is believed to have them. Whoever possesses wealth attracts the covetous regard of others. It is unimportant that others desire something that is unworthy of being desired; what matters is the covetous regard itself. It is this regard that each of us avidly seeks for himself, without knowing it. An economy, then, is a sucker's game, a piece of theater in which each player is at once a dupe and a party to his own deception. It is, in other words, an immense lie that we tell to ourselves, a collective exercise in self-deceit.

What is this author's name, and what is the title of the work I have in mind? One might be forgiven for supposing the author to be Alexis de Tocqueville. After all, it was Tocqueville, in a delightful chapter of the second volume of *Democracy in America* (1840), "Why Americans Are So Restless in the Midst of Their Well-Being," who noted that "a materialist philosophy is virtually unknown to them, although their passion for material well-being is general."[11] From what I have already said, however, the reader knows that the author did not write in French. Nor, as it turns out, did he write in the nineteenth century.

I have laid a trap: the author of the chapter in question, entitled "Of the Nature of Self-Deceit" in the original English, is known today not only as an economist, but as the founding father of modern economics. He is none other than Adam Smith, about whom the most arrant nonsense has been written for more than three hundred years. And yet at the time he composed *The Theory of Moral Sentiments*, in 1759, he was not yet the economist he was to become over the course of the next two decades while composing *An Inquiry into the Nature and Causes of the Wealth of Nations*, published in 1776. Smith started out as a moral philosopher, teaching at Glasgow, and became a foremost representative of the Scottish Enlightenment. His *Theory*—the womb from which, as Smith himself insisted, the *Inquiry* sprang—remains the most complete statement of his thinking about man and society.

Wealth, he holds, attracts the envious notice of others, because they wish to be wealthy themselves; and if they desire wealth, it is so that they themselves may be noticed in their turn. The poor man suffers less from being poor than from the fact that no one pays attention to him.

If, then, by contrast with the earliest sense of the word *economy*, in which one has a foretaste of the legendary stinginess of the Scottish (summed up in English by the verb "to economize," in French by the phrase "faire des économies"), the discipline of economics contemplates an extravagant future of unlimited growth still today, it is because economic behavior is motivated much less by needs than by desire. With only rare exceptions, the history of economic thought since Adam Smith has been one of neglect—of forgetting, or perhaps repressing, this fundamental insight. Since economic behavior itself amounts to self-deceit on a vast scale, it should come as no surprise that economic theory should participate in the same grand illusion. This is the crucial connection I mentioned earlier, between domain and point of view, between social reality and the perception of it, that is captured in French by the word *l'économie* and in English by the new term I have suggested, Economy.

We must therefore begin to think about Economy by repudiating the discipline that has taken from it both its name and its object of study. But we must also listen to economists very closely when they speak. It is no contradiction of what I have just said to acknowledge that neoclassical economic theory has produced works of prodigious ingenuity, even brilliance. Liars, and particularly ones who lie to themselves, are often the most skillful sophists. In carefully parsing the language of bad faith spoken by economists, we will learn more about the hidden truths of Economy than by accepting at face value the claim of economists to have explained the world as it really is.

CHAPTER 1

Economy and the Problem of Evil

Evil is never "radical," it is only extreme; it possesses neither depth nor any demonic dimension. It can overgrow and lay waste the whole world precisely because it spreads like a fungus on the surface. It is "thought-defying," because thought tries to reach some depth, to go to the roots, and the moment it concerns itself with evil, it is frustrated because *there is nothing.* That is its "banality."

—Hannah Arendt, letter to Gershom Scholem, 20 July 1963

There is no better way to understand how Economy has come to take up an unreasonably large place in our lives than to begin by considering the sense in which it constitutes a solution to the problem of evil. Just as the history of modern philosophy can be interpreted as a succession of replies given to this problem,[1] so too the history of modern economic thought can be regarded as having followed a parallel course.

There was a time, not so very long ago, when human beings believed that death, sickness, and accidental injury are rightfully inflicted by God on all who sin against Him, in accordance with the principle of the *summum bonum*, or the highest good, which God's perfection obliges him to bring about. On this view, God is the cause of physical evil. The question arose, then, whether He is also the cause of sin and of moral evil; and, if so, how He could have invented the very thing that corrupts His creation. The attempt to vindicate God's will was called theodicy in Greek, and it is this term that is traditionally used to refer to all human attempts to justify the existence of evil in a world that has been perfectly made.

Theodicies Old and New

Saint Augustine's answer to the question is well known: God did not wish for moral evil to be; but He could not have done otherwise than to permit it, for, in creating man in His image, He created him free, and therefore free to choose evil. This argument was widely attacked. The most formidable assault came from the Calvinist philosopher and theologian Pierre Bayle, author of a monumental *Historical and Critical Dictionary* (1695–97). If I wish to make a gift to my enemies, Bayle mockingly retorted, nothing is easier than to give them something that will bring about their downfall. The German philosopher and mathematician Gottfried Wilhelm Leibniz undertook to defend Augustine against Bayle in a pair of works that form the twin pillars of his metaphysics: the first, published in French in 1710, was a volume of essays on the goodness of God, the freedom of man, and the origin of evil titled *Theodicy*; the second, the *Monadology*, followed four years later.

Leibniz argued that God's understanding comprehends an infinity of possible worlds. In deciding which one of these to bring into existence, He was prevented from choosing arbitrarily by the principle of sufficient reason, which requires that every effect have a cause. What is more, God could only choose the best world, again by virtue of the principle of the *summum bonum*, from which it follows that only that which displays the greatest possible degree of perfection can exist. Does this principle of the best, as it is also known, mean that God could not have chosen otherwise? No, for the necessity that guided his decision was only moral, and not metaphysical; in other words, there would not have been any logical contradiction in God's choosing another world than the best one. Yet in order to bring about the best of all possible worlds, God was obliged to leave some measure of evil in it; without this residuum our world would have been less perfect overall, since in that case it could be improved in one way only on pain of making it still worse in some other way. Everything that appears as evil from the finite point of view of the individual monad is, from the point of view of the totality of all sentient beings, a necessary sacrifice for the greatest good of the totality. Evil is therefore only an illusion, a mere perspectival effect. Leibniz's theodicy is the source of utilitarianism in moral philosophy, and his monadology the source of Adam Smith's theory of the invisible hand.[2]

The doctrine of metaphysical optimism, as this version of theodicy is also known (where "optimism" has its classical sense, referring to the best possible state of affairs rather than a hopeful attitude toward the future), was shattered on 1 November 1755 by an earthquake of scarcely less great magnitude than that of the Sumatra earthquake 250 years later. The raging fires that came after, in Lisbon and elsewhere, were extinguished finally by a gigantic tsunami that unleashed waves fifteen meters high as far away as the shores of Morocco. The Portuguese capital was annihilated. From this catastrophe there issued two views of evil, which came to be associated with the names of Voltaire and Rousseau, respectively. In March 1756, Voltaire published a philosophical essay in verse, *Poem on the Lisbon Disaster*, to which Rousseau replied with a *Letter to Monsieur de Voltaire*, dated 18 August of the same year.

Voltaire, adopting a position it is tempting in hindsight to call "postmodern," asked his readers to accept the pure contingency of events and to admit that the chain of causes and effects can never fully be explained. Rousseau, for his part, denied that God punishes men for their sins, and argued that a human, quasi-scientific explanation could be found for such catastrophes. Seven years afterward, in *Émile* (1762), he drew the lesson of the Lisbon disaster: "Man, seek the author of evil no longer. It is yourself. No evil exists other than that which you do or suffer, and both come to you from yourself."[3]

Proof of Rousseau's triumph is to be found in the world's reaction to two of the greatest natural disasters in recent memory: the Asian tsunami of Christmas 2004 and Hurricane Katrina in August of the following year. For it was precisely their status as *natural* catastrophes that contemporary accounts rejected. The *New York Times* reported news of the hurricane under the headline "A Man-Made Disaster." The same thing had already been said about the tsunami, and with good reason: had Thailand's coral reefs and coastal mangroves not been severely eroded by urbanization, tourism, aquaculture, and climate change, they would have slowed the advance of the deadly tidal wave and significantly reduced the scope of the disaster. In New Orleans, as it turned out, the levees constructed to protect the city had not been properly maintained for many years, and troops of the Louisiana National Guard who might have helped after the storm were unavailable because they had been called up for duty in Iraq. The same people who later questioned the wisdom of building a city on marshland next to the sea now wonder why the Japanese should have thought they could safely develop civilian nuclear power, since geography condemned them to do this in seismic zones vulnerable to massive flooding. The lesson, they say, is plain: humanity, and only humanity, is responsible (if not also to blame) for the misfortunes that beset it.

This human evil Rousseau called *amour-propre*, which he contrasted with *amour de soi*. I have shown elsewhere that Adam Smith's concept of "self-love" is to be interpreted in exactly the sense of Rousseau's *amour-propre*, and not as what Rousseau meant by *amour de soi*.[4] In the *Dialogues*, the most revealing work that he left us concerning *amour-propre* (also known as *Rousseau, Judge of Jean-Jacques*, a sequel to the *Confessions*, in effect, published in 1776), Rousseau wrote:

> The primitive passions, which all tend directly toward our happiness, focus us only on objects that relate to it, and having only *amour de soi* as a principle, are all loving and gentle in their essence. But when, being *deflected from their object by obstacles, they focus on removing the obstacle rather than on reaching the object*; then they change nature and become irascible and hateful. And that is how *amour de soi*, which is a good and absolute feeling, becomes *amour-propre*, which is to say a relative feeling by which one makes comparisons; the latter feeling demands preferences, and *its enjoyment is purely negative, as it no longer seeks satisfaction in our own benefit but solely in the harm of another*.[5]

Amour-propre is a destructive force, the malign offspring of *amour de soi*: it is when personal interests collide ("cross each other," Rousseau says), that *amour de soi* changes into *amour-propre*.[6] The transformation occurs when one person's gaze crosses another's, giving rise in turn to the sidelong glance—the invidious look (Latin *invidia*, from the verbal form meaning "to cast an evil eye upon"). It is by means of envy, then, that *amour de soi* is converted into jealousy and resentment, creating a spirit of animosity whose blind determination to overcome everything that stands in its way causes it to relinquish all claim to rationality.

The great moral horrors of the twentieth century brought into existence a new order of evil that was the exact opposite of the one Rousseau had described. Vladimir Jankélévitch called Rousseau's conception an "anthropodicy," which is to say a theodicy in which man is substituted for God. In the new conception, the primacy of God (or "nature") was restored, to the point that it now became possible to speak of the *naturalization* of evil.

In 1958, the German philosopher Günther Anders traveled to Hiroshima and Nagasaki to take part in the Fourth World Conference against Atomic and Hydrogen Bombs. After many conversations with survivors of the catastrophe, he noted in his diary: "Their steadfast resolve not to speak of those who were to blame, not to say that the event had been caused by human beings; not to harbor the least resentment, even though they were the victims of the greatest of crimes—this really is too much for me, it passes all understanding." And he added: "They constantly speak of the catastrophe as if it were an earthquake or a tidal wave. They use the Japanese word, *tsunami*."[7]

Anders succeeded in identifying this new regime of evil at about the same time as Hannah Arendt (a fellow student at Marburg, and also his first wife). Arendt spoke of Auschwitz, Anders of Hiroshima. Whereas Arendt diagnosed Eichmann's psychological disability as a "lack of imagination,"[8] Anders showed that this is not the weakness of any one person in particular; it is the weakness of every person when mankind's capacity for invention, and for destruction, becomes disproportionately enlarged in relation to the human condition. In that case evil acquires an autonomy of its own in relation to the intentions of those who commit it. Anders and Arendt each drew attention to a scandalous paradox, namely, that immense harm may be caused without the least malevolence; that unimaginable guilt may go hand in hand with an utter absence of malice. Once our moral categories have been robbed of their power to describe and judge evil, when evil exceeds our powers of comprehension, when it becomes inconceivable, one must be prepared to say, with the jurist Yosal Rogat, that "a great crime offends nature, so that the very earth cries out for vengeance; that evil violates a natural harmony which only retribution can restore; that a wronged collectivity owes a duty to the moral order to punish the criminal."[9] That European Jews should have replaced "holocaust" with the Hebrew word *shoah*, which signifies a natural catastrophe (in particular, a flood or tidal wave), tells us how strong the temptation to naturalize evil can be when human beings find themselves incapable of grasping the horror of the very thing they have done or had done to them.

We are now in a position to consider Economy in its relation to the problem of evil. The great sociologist Émile Durkheim, in his last major work, *The Elementary Forms of Religious Life* (1912), took credit for a result that the anthropology of his time had made virtually a commonplace: "I have established that the fundamental categories of thought, and consequently of science, have religious origins. This is true of magic as well, and of the various techniques derived from it. On the other hand, it has long been known that until a relatively advanced period in evolution, the rules of morality and law were indistinguishable from ritual prescriptions. In short, then, it can be said that *nearly all* great social institutions are born of religion."[10] This "nearly all" comes as a surprise. A footnote explains its meaning:

> Only one form of social activity has not yet been explicitly linked to religion: namely, economic activity. However, techniques derived from magic are found, by that very fact, to have indirectly religious origins. Moreover, economic value is a kind of power, of efficacy, and we know the religious origins of the idea of power. Wealth can confer *mana*; this is how it comes to have it. In this way, we see that the idea of economic value and that of religious value cannot be unrelated. But the nature of these relationships has not yet been studied.[11]

My work over the past thirty years in social and political philosophy has been guided by the conviction not only that Economy cannot be explained without reference to religion, but that Economy occupies the place emptied out by the desacralization the world, itself an eminently religious phenomenon. The recent economic crisis must therefore be placed in the long perspective of modernity, beginning in the seventeenth century.

Economic Violence

Media commentary about the sudden collapse of the global economy that began with the panic of August 2007 often uses words like "earthquake" or "tsunami"—so often, in fact, that no one even notices. There is nevertheless something shocking *and* profoundly true about likening a moral catastrophe of this scope to a natural catastrophe. We would do well to think about it with some care.

When a great wave rises up suddenly from the depths of the sea and radiates with lightning speed until it crashes against sleeping shores with unimaginable force, it chooses neither those whom it carries away nor those whom it spares. One thinks of Voltaire's famous lines, heaping scorn on theodicy after the Lisbon earthquake in 1755:

> Leibniz can't tell me from what secret cause
> In a world governed by the wisest laws,
> Lasting disorders, woes that never end
> With our vain pleasures real sufferings blend;
> Why ill the virtuous with the vicious shares?
> Why neither good nor bad misfortune spares?[12]

Today, some of the worst swindlers have paid for their crimes, or will pay one day, but organizations devoted to the public good whose only mistake was to place their confidence in them have had to pay as well. Other crooks are sure to emerge from the crisis unscathed, however, whereas well-managed and once flourishing companies will have gone under. The evil that strikes the world is blind and without purpose, as we are forced to admit—joining Voltaire in acknowledging, too, that we are at a loss to understand why:

> I can't conceive that "what is, ought to be,"
> In this each doctor knows as much as me.[13]

Voltaire's courage and lucidity, both, are lacking among the two classes of experts who comment most prominently on the crisis: those who cling, pigheadedly, in the face of all evidence to the contrary, to the doctrine of efficient markets; and those at the opposite end of the ideological spectrum, equally incapable of regarding capitalism as anything other than omniscient and omnipotent, who imagine it to be a conspiracy by the powerful to further enrich themselves while continuing to exploit the poor. In searching for an explanation where none is to be found, both sides desperately seek to reassure themselves that all is well.

Not the least of the things that the crisis destroyed is the notion that human behavior is shaped by incentives, long one of the pillars of neoclassical economic theory. Few free-market theorists believe that the decisions of the market are fair; most of them, beginning with John Rawls, hold that they are neither just nor unjust, that these predicates are meaningless. The valuations arrived at by the market are indifferent to merit, indifferent to moral worth, indifferent to human needs. Consider the case of a hardworking doctor who is honest, poor, and less skilled than other doctors. Is it unjust that he will be put out of business by his competitors? Justice has nothing to do with it: the rules are the same for everyone; the process is anonymous, bereft of intention, undirected by any personal will. The same theorists generally accept, however, that there is a discernible connection between individual actions and the decisions of the market that *encourages* each agent to make reasonable choices, which, in the aggregate, will tend to promote the common good. Thus the incompetent physician, forced to change his profession, will discover his true calling and put his talents to better use. It is this link, between what a person does and how the market responds, that the present crisis has destroyed—or, still worse, has shown to be illusory. It is as though economic agents are no more than marionettes, at the mercy of the whims of hidden divinities. The present crisis is therefore, at bottom, a crisis of meaning. The confusion it has caused is total.

Economic violence is not a recent discovery. The Marxian analysis of Economy in its capitalist form, and particularly the concepts of alienation and exploitation, are more valuable today than ever. As for the Communist variant of Economy, its terrifying malignancy is proved by the history of the twentieth century itself. Even the greatest liberal economists recognized that economic competition is nasty, brutal, and long-lasting in its effects. Adam Smith went so far as to say that it was responsible for "the corruption of the Moral Sentiments."[14] Keynes examined the conditions under which an economy may become locked in states that are harmful for all actors, where unemployment and shrinking investment opportunities reinforce each other instead of triggering a return to full-employment equilibrium.[15] More recent critiques are no less forceful or pertinent. Members of the Frankfurt School, Ivan Illich, political ecologists such as André Gorz, and Heidegger's "children" (notably Hannah Arendt, Günther Anders, and Hans Jonas) have all illuminated important aspects of economic violence.

Economy and Violence

All the things I have just mentioned are well known. What is not well known is that there was a time when more, rather than less, economic competition was considered to be the only way societies in the throes of desacralization could be protected against their own violence. The extraordinary thing is that the arguments advanced to justify this claim were in large part the very ones that critics of Economy later put forward to condemn it, as the historian Albert Hirschman demonstrated in an influential book, *The Passions and the Interests* (1977). Hirschman recounts the birth, ascendency, and eclipse of an idea: that economic self-interest—the private pursuit of the greatest possible material gain—operates to restrain the passions favoring reckless behavior and promoting discord, antagonism, and armed hostility. In a society riven by civil strife and foreign wars, unable any longer to look outside itself for the moral authority it once found in religion, the idea that economic activity could curb destructive impulses arose from a need to contrive a substitute for the sacred, a means of disciplining individual misbehavior and staving off social disintegration.

The irony that lay in wait was complete: "Capitalism," Hirschman observes, "was supposed to accomplish exactly what was soon to be denounced as its worst feature."[16] The impoverishment of social life, reduced to a mere talent for calculating economic advantage; the isolation of individuals from one another and the predictability of their behavior—in short, everything that in our time has been held responsible for the alienation of workers from the products of their labor in capitalist society was welcomed as a way of putting an end to murderous, and ultimately pathetic, struggles for power, grandeur, and fame. Mutual indifference and a selfish preoccupation with personal affairs—thus the remedies that were once imagined to be indispensable if the *contagion* of violent passions were to be arrested, as Hirschman reminds us by looking at the writings of Montesquieu and leading figures of the Scottish Enlightenment, above all James Steuart and David Hume.

Nevertheless it was in the work of one of the most influential social philosophers of the twentieth century, Keynes's great adversary Friedrich Hayek, that the economistic interpretation of these ideas was to be most strikingly formulated. No matter that he was awarded the Nobel Prize in Economics toward the end of his career, Hayek remained a marginal figure in the profession, looked down upon by neoclassical economists (even more than by Keynesians) because he rejected the traditional interpretation of the Walrasian model in terms of equilibrium and optimality. Instead he insisted upon the need for a general surrender to "the blind forces of the social process"[17]—exactly what I referred to earlier as the unmeaningfulness, the nonsensicalness of Economy! For Hayek, however, this surrender is the indispensable condition of freedom, efficiency, justice, and social peace.

In a way that sometimes curiously recalls Rousseau, the first of the great "constructivists" whom he sought to combat, Hayek argues that evil arises from the tyranny of personal dependence, the submission of one person to another's arbitrary will. This state of subordination can be escaped only if every member of society willingly subjects himself to an abstract, impersonal, and universal rule that absolutely transcends him. Whereas Rousseau's laws of social life have the same inflexibility and the same exteriority as the laws of nature, Hayek's laws of the market are still more rigid and more indecipherable, since social complexity propels individuals onto a course whose direction they can neither change nor foresee.

That direction is nevertheless the right one, Hayek maintains. The idea that the market may be efficient even in the absence of incentives is his chief contribution to the model of general equilibrium, though, as I say, the majority of economists remain unpersuaded. To appreciate the full force of Hayek's arguments it would be necessary to set them in the context of his theory of cultural evolution and selection, a considerable task that lies beyond the scope of the present work.[18] It is clear enough, however, why Hayek should hold that submitting to anonymous rules and forces, which transcend us even though we have produced them ourselves, is unavoidable if justice and social peace are to be achieved: doing so removes all grounds for resentment, envy, and the other destructive passions. A person whom the market punishes by depriving him of his job, his business, even his means of subsistence, knows full well that no one wished this to happen to him. Accordingly, Hayek says, he suffers no humiliation.[19]

Here we recognize the outstanding feature of the new regime of evil that Arendt, Anders, and others since have described in connection with Hiroshima, Auschwitz, nuclear deterrence, and so-called NBIC convergence (the convergence of nanotechnology, biotechnology, information technology, and cognitive science)—only now the evil has become the good. It would be more accurate, however, to say that this regime of *self-transcendence*, as Hayek called it,[20] sometimes involves a new form of the good, associated with a distinctive conception of friendship (*philia*), and sometimes a new form of evil, the unspeakable, whose origins lie within us. We are dealing here, then, with what may be called the *ambivalence* of evil. Is Economy a source of violence, as a long line of authors from Marx to present-day critics of capitalism would have it? Or is it a bulwark against violence, as a still longer liberal tradition extending from Montesquieu to Hayek asserts? Is Economy, in other words, remedy or poison?

Economy and the Sacred

Thirty years ago, while rereading Adam Smith, I saw a way to resolve this dilemma. At the same moment I discovered the work of René Girard.

My interpretation of the great Scottish philosopher-economist's thinking can be summed up by a formula that is something more than a facile play on words. It occurred to me in the course of devising a novel solution to the "Adam Smith Problem," that is, the apparent contradiction between his two major works, *The Theory of Moral Sentiments* and the *Inquiry into the Wealth of Nations.* For Smith, Economy *contains* violence—in both senses of this word. Economy has violence in it; it is, if you like, inherently violent. But it also acts as a barrier against violence. It is as if violence finds in commerce and industry the means of limiting itself, and therefore of protecting the social order against collapse. The ambivalence of economic life in relation to evil, in other words, exactly mirrors the ambivalence of the sacred in relation to violence.

Again, as in the case of Hayek, I must refer the reader to one of my earlier works for a complete exegesis.[21] For the moment it will be enough to make the following points. One often—too often—hears it said that Smith was the father of political economy, for having elaborated a theory of what is generally called the natural harmony of interests.[22] Individuals moved solely by "selfish interests" and animated by self-love produce economic prosperity and social harmony without either knowing it or wishing it, as though they were manipulated by an "invisible hand." Smith's philosophy is therefore seen to stand in a direct line of descent from the tradition analyzed by Hirschman—except that now passions have disappeared from the picture.[23]

This, I believe, is a grave error of interpretation, and one that has been propagated over time in the same way that legends are propagated. It would be truer to say that Smith regards interests as having been contaminated by destructive passions, which they contain in the two senses of the word I have just indicated. To use Rousseau's terms, one loves oneself through *amour-propre*, not through *amour de soi*. This means that improvement of our economic circumstances—bettering our condition, in Smith's phrase—depends on being able to attract the "sympathy" of others: if we desire wealth, it is not for the illusory material satisfactions that it may give; it is because wealth brings us the admiration of others, an admiration fatally tinged by envy. Inevitably, then, the price of public prosperity is the corruption of our moral sentiments.

The reader may well imagine the immensity of the intellectual shock I experienced on becoming acquainted at the same moment with René Girard's anthropology of violence and the sacred. At the heart of his theory I detected the same structure in the form of a paradox: through the sacred, violence distances itself from itself in order to curb its own power. As the gospel account (Mark 3:23) puts it, Satan casts out Satan.

In reviving a long tradition of religious anthropology interrupted by the Second World War and the decades of structuralism and "deconstructionist" poststructuralism that followed, Girard seeks to renew inquiry into the origins of culture. Like Durkheim, Mauss, Freud, Frazer, Hocart, and others before him, he considers that culture arose in conjunction with the notion of the sacred. Girard's "hypothesis" (his own term) suggests that the sacred was produced by a mechanism of self-externalization, so that violence, in projecting itself beyond the domain of human control by means of ritual practices and systems of rules, prohibitions, and obligations, became self-limiting. On this view, the sacred is identified with a "good" form of institutionalized violence that holds in check "bad" anarchic violence.[24] The desacralization of the world that modernity brought about is built upon a kind of knowledge, or suspicion perhaps, that gradually insinuated itself in human thinking— the suspicion that good and bad violence are not opposites, but actually one and the same; that, at bottom, there is no difference between them. This knowledge, hidden since the foundation of the world, as Girard puts it, was revealed to us by the Passion of Christ and the accounts and interpretations of it that have been given to us in the New Testament.

This is not the place to discuss the hypothesis itself. What I wish to examine here is a question that Girard's anthropology poses but fails to answer. Revelation, it holds, has worked over the centuries to destroy the effectiveness of sacrificial systems, with the result that we now find ourselves left to face our own violence alone. This is the diabolical trick that Christianity has played on mankind—and why Christianity seemed so dangerous to thinkers like Machiavelli. How, then, are we to account for the fact that humanity itself has not, or has not yet, suffered the fate to which uncountably many societies since the beginning of human history have fallen victim: self-annihilation through internecine violence?

To this question I replied, in a book written more than thirty years ago with the Canadian philosopher Paul Dumouchel,[25] that economic activity represents a continuation of the sacred: like the sacred, it blocks violence through violence, only the means it employs are altogether different. Certainly this is what led Hegel to ascribe so much importance to the particular needs associated with a market economy, which he considered to be essential to the spiritual development of mankind.

Economic Self-Transcendence and Panic

I mentioned earlier that one finds the figure of self-transcendence in both economic thought and in the social philosophy of thinkers, such as Hayek, who are inspired by economic thought.[26] But it is never presented in the form that I have just given it. Evil is not seen to contain itself through self-transcendence. Instead, good is supposed to contain evil (and the end the means) while at the same time exploiting it, as a necessary evil in a sense, in keeping with the classic schema of theodicy. Bernard de Mandeville's formula "Private Vices, Publick Benefits"[27]—long regarded as the earliest statement of free-market ideology—is a fine illustration of this style of thinking. One thinks, too, of the way Goethe describes Mephistopheles in his *Faust*:

> Part of that Power which would
> Do evil constantly and constantly does good.[28]

The logical structure in either case is a hierarchical opposition in which the higher level contradicts the lower level from which it emerges. This manner of picturing their relationship has the disadvantage, however, of obscuring the crucial fact that the two levels are the same.

Notwithstanding its great mathematical abstraction, the economic model of general equilibrium due to Léon Walras and his many successors exhibits an identical structure. It is this model that is being criticized today every time the public is told that the crisis shattered once and for all the myth that markets are self-regulating, which is to say that they spontaneously find a path to equilibrium. From this, of course, it is concluded that they need to be regulated by some other means. No better example of the incoherence that muddles economic thinking can be found: category errors abound. The same people who now make this argument used to say that the self-regulating market is a sign of the alienation that characterizes modern industrial society, since a self-regulating market is one that, by definition, has no need of human control. The denunciation of market autonomy in a capitalist system as something contrary to democratic principles is then suddenly stood on its head, and the same system is rebuked for its failure to be self-organizing.

What has to be understood in all of this is that the market, and more broadly the economy as a whole, is indeed capable of regulating itself—only self-regulation occurs through the apparently paradoxical emergence from within of an external form of authority, founded on prices. What is more, the consequences of this state of affairs are liable to be disastrous from the point of view of efficiency and justice. Whether it continues to function under all conditions, even during periods of speculative euphoria, or whether it breaks down under the pressures of investor panic, the market is in any case self-regulating. This is one of its essential properties, which it shares with all complex systems, by the virtue of the fact that effects feed back on causes: it regulates its own behavior in creating a mechanism of external control, in the form of forces that seem to economic agents to impose their will on them, whereas in fact these forces result from the synergistic coordination of individual behaviors.[29] The category error that must be avoided here is confusing a value judgment about what the market does to the human beings who act on it, and who are subject to its effects, with an objective analysis of the self-organizing structure of the market and its functional dynamics. Self-regulation may be good or bad, but either way it is self-regulation.

Let me explain exactly what I mean when I say that self-regulation occurs through the internal production of an exteriority, what I call self-transcendence. In its simplest form, this external vantage point is constituted by prices and the movement of prices, which agents take to be given, as though they were a sort of fact of nature, whereas agents themselves are the ones who bring prices into the world, the offspring, as it were, of their own infinitely entangled decisions. Keynes's genius was to see that businessmen's expectations govern the distribution of incomes, and therefore the level of consumer demand. In the case where pessimism is universal, for example, where employers take it for granted that they will not find buyers and workers take it for granted that they will not find employment (and therefore will be unable to buy), expectations become not only self-fulfilling but mutually reinforcing, locking the economy in a deflationary spiral whose absurdity does not prevent it from spreading misery all around.

Market self-transcendence is the way Satan casts out Satan in economic life: good violence holds bad violence at bay. Nevertheless, this is the point I wish once again to emphasize—they are, at bottom, the same violence. Virtually all commentators on the recent crisis set good in opposition to one kind of evil or another, with the aim of showing that the evil in question is, at best, a necessary evil placed in the service of the public interest. Thus the so-called real economy is set against the financial economy, regulated markets against speculative markets, bullish buying against bearish short-selling, and so on. Distinguishing categories in this fashion allows some of them to be singled out for blame—depending on the case, and in order of increasing specificity: the financial economy, speculative markets, bearish speculation, and so on. Rationalist analysis of the crisis, in other words, offers reassurance by separating the guilty from the innocent. But these are false distinctions. If we wish to see the matter clearly, we must look for similarities where everyone else persists in seeing differences.

The financial economy is generally supposed to be evil because it breeds speculation, and therefore illusion; it stands in opposition to the real economy, which, by contrast, is solid and dependable. The word "speculation" comes from the Latin *speculum*, meaning mirror. In what sense does financial speculation hold up a mirror to our behavior? Speculation consists in buying a good, not because one wishes to hold on to it indefinitely, but because one counts on being able to sell it to someone who desires it still more. The mirror in this case is the gaze that another person casts on a good that one looks to acquire. In the world of finance, the relevant good is typically an accounting entry: a value, a share, a bond, a security, a currency. Yet the real economy, even if it deals in goods and services having an undoubtedly material character, exhibits essentially the same logic: we desire a commodity because the desire of another person to possess it makes us aware of its desirability. Recall once again Adam Smith's insight. Wealth, Smith says, is that which is desired by the person whose regard we seek to attract—our *spectator*.[30] Because both economies display a specular logic, any *normative* opposition is untenable.

Like the sacred before it, Economy is rapidly losing its power to produce self-limiting rules, rules that limit its own violence. This is the true meaning of the crisis. Greek mythology gave a name to what happens when a hierarchy (in its etymological sense, a sacred order) collapses on itself: panic. In a panic, the mechanism of self-transcendence still continues to operate, as we will see in chapter 2; but it no longer has the crucial capacity for self-limitation. Instead panic absorbs every outside force that threatens to raise a barrier against it. When one hears the world's great bankers solemnly pledge to rebuild the international financial system through more stringent and effective regulation, or even, a still more grandiose ambition, to remake capitalism itself, it is impossible not to be reminded of the third scene of act 2 of Molière's *Bourgeois Gentleman*. From the commanding heights of his magisterium, the philosophy master attempts to arbitrate between the competing claims of the music master, the dancing master, and the fencing master, each of whom demands that his art be recognized as the best one of all. But it is not long before he begins to squabble, and then to fight, with them, so that what had been a dispute among three parties swiftly escalates into a war among four.

Today the bankers' arrogance comes from imagining that they can, like Napoleon, crown themselves emperor—pretend to be their own master, occupying a position of ultimate authority in relation to themselves. The consequences of this imperial fantasy are plain for all to see: at the height of the crisis, financial authorities injected astronomical quantities of liquidity into the global banking system, in order to reassure the markets; but in doing so they produced exactly the opposite effect, for the markets concluded that only panic could explain why it should be necessary to resort to such extreme measures. The markets, in other words, did not for a moment believe in the proclaimed rationality of state intervention. To speak of reconstructing capitalism through renewed market regulation is therefore a staggering piece of naïveté, for it supposes that the underlying problem, of compensating for the disappearance of an external source of authority, has already been solved. In taking up all the space there is, within and without, Economy has sealed its own fate.

The Contamination of Ethics by Economy

Some commentators speak of making capitalism "more ethical" by increasing the incentives for honest behavior and instructing financial traders, in particular, in their social responsibilities. But it is too late—ethics has already been bewildered and bamboozled as well. It would be like adding a few drops of mineral water to a glass of tap water.

In the same way that an economy is self-organizing even when it is about to plunge headlong over the cliff, it provides itself with its own ethical guidance even when it produces a world that will soon be unlivable. A market economy is driven by competition, and the effects of competition are apt to be very harsh: some people cannot find work, others lose their jobs; firms are abandoned by longtime customers and go bankrupt; disappointed investors go for broke and lose everything; new products sink without a trace despite years of research and development. All these failures seem to come of the blue, like so many unpredictable and incomprehensible strokes of fate. Paradoxically, it is just this, in Hayek's world, that makes such suffering bearable: no one wished for these things to happen. In the real world, however, they cause humiliation, indignation, and, more and more often today, despair.

Economy nevertheless persists in seeing itself as the antidote to the very poison that it distills. There is no plainer statement of this opinion than the panegyric to the market composed by Milton Friedman: "Adam Smith's flash of genius was his recognition that the prices that emerged from voluntary transactions between buyers and sellers—for short, in a free market—could coordinate the activity of millions of people, each seeking his own interest, in such a way as to make everyone better off. . . . The price system is the mechanism that performs this task without central direction, *without requiring people to speak to one another or to like one another.*"[31] This bizarre utopia—a society in which people have no need of friendship, or even of conversation, in order to live in peace with one another, in which mutual indifference and solipsistic amusements are the surest guarantees of the common good—is so monstrous that it could only have been conceived, and, what is more, could have only been taken seriously by a great many brilliant minds, for a very compelling reason. The reason, I believe, is this.

From Rousseau we know that evil appears when our passions, having been "deflected from their object by obstacles," are redirected for the purpose of "removing the obstacle rather than reaching the object." The obstacle is a rival, the person or thing that stands between me and the object of my desire. In a world of unrestrained competition, rivals are to be found everywhere. Tocqueville described this state of affairs with admirable clarity in connection with democratic societies, which is to say societies that are characterized by equality of opportunity:

> When all the privileges of birth and wealth are destroyed, when all the professions are open to all, and when a man can climb to the top of any of them through his own merits, men's ambitions think that they see before them a great and open career and readily imagine they are summoned to no common destiny. Such, however, is a mistaken view which experience corrects daily. This very equality which allows each citizen to imagine unlimited hopes makes all of them weak as individuals. It restricts their strength on every side while offering freer scope to their longings.
>
> Not only are they powerless by themselves but at every step they encounter *immense obstacles* unnoticed at first sight.
>
> They have abolished the troublesome privileges of a few of their fellow men only to *meet the competition of all.* The barrier has changed shape

rather than place. Once men are more or less equal and pursue the same path, it is very difficult for any one of them to move forward quickly in order to cleave his way through the uniform crowd milling around him.

This permanent struggle between the instincts inspired by equality and the means it supplies to satisfy them harasses and wearies men's minds.

And a bit further on:

However democratic the state of society and the nation's political constitution, you can guarantee that each citizen will always spot several oppressive points near to him and you may anticipate that he *will direct his gaze doggedly in that direction.* When inequality is the general law of society, the most blatant inequalities escape notice; when everything is virtually on a level, the slightest variations cause distress. That is why the desire for equality becomes more insatiable as equality extends to all.[32]

In societies founded on the principle of equality, rivals are everywhere—and all rivals are obstacles. Evil is met with in losing sight of one's purpose, and then in concentrating one's energies exclusively on sweeping aside whatever stands in one's way. This fascination with obstacles is nowhere more intensely felt than in sexual competition, but it would be foolish to think that it does not occur in economic competition as well. The business press supplies us with a wealth of new examples every week. What Dostoyevsky (here the perfect disciple of Rousseau) identified as the psychology of the "underground" is all the greater a threat to Economy as it constantly works to undermine our interest in cooperating with others.

The passage from Friedman I quoted a moment ago amounts to the economist's solution to this problem. Since the evil of competition arises from an obsessive concern with eliminating the obstacle presented by a rival who is at once admired and detested, the simplest remedy is to completely separate economic agents from one another: war can now be waged without the combatants ever having to meet face-to-face. On this view of the matter, the model of general equilibrium can be seen as an elaborate device for unleashing the forces of competition while limiting the harm that agents can cause one another. The paradox of belligerent isolationism, as it might be called, is not very far removed from the chilling prophecy of Günther

Anders, who foresaw the advent of an earthly paradise "inhabited by murderers without malice and victims without hatred."[33]

But how can there be competition if there is no rivalry? And how can there be rivalry if desire has not already been aroused? The moment desire makes its appearance, as Adam Smith well understood, all the bad passions—envy, jealousy, resentment—immediately and inescapably come into play. To suppose otherwise is to ignore what happens in the real world. However appealing the ethical doctrine implicit in neoclassical economic theory may seem, if only for its simplicity, making avoidance and abstraction the answer to the problem of limiting the violence of destructive passions raises a troubling question: must human beings be transformed first into zombies if they are to be able to protect themselves against the evil that rises up from underground?

CHAPTER 2

Self-Transcendence

As part of society, the individual naturally transcends himself, both when he thinks and when he acts.

—Émile Durkheim, *The Elementary Forms of Religious Life*

I t was in the course of examining the parallel destinies of economic theory and philosophy in relation to the problem of evil that we first encountered the concept of self-transcendence. As it happens, this same concept—even if it is not part of the usual repertoire of economists—is indispensable to an understanding of how market mechanisms operate. The notion of an invisible hand alone is not enough: a market is able to be self-organizing because it undergoes a process of self-transcendence, by projecting itself outside of itself. This exteriority assumes the form of something that each agent takes to be fixed and independent of what he thinks or does, although in fact it results from the synergistic interaction of his own behavior with that of others. The system of prices is the most obvious example, but there is another, much more subtle one, which we are accustomed to call the future. The market is pulled forward by an idea of what has not yet happened that it projects in front of itself, like a mountain climber who ascends a smooth, ice-covered slope by throwing his pick ahead of him and pulling himself up to a new height. This image nonetheless lacks an essential element, in which the paradox of the self-transcendence of the future resides. Times to come cannot be said to resemble the face of a mountain since, by definition, they have no present existence. And yet the market acts as though it were able to give a kind of reality to what does not yet exist. For the ice-covered face of a mountain we must therefore substitute the image of Baron Münchausen, who claimed to have pulled himself out of a swamp by his own hair.[1]

Man stands apart from the other animals because he is able, in Nietzsche's phrase, "to see and anticipate distant eventualities as if they belonged to the present."[2] Whether or not market behavior represents the highest expression of this ability, as I am inclined to believe, the power to anticipate events is far from being the dry abstraction assumed by neoclassical economic theory without further explanation. The crises of capitalism, as John Maynard Keynes was the first to appreciate, are essentially crises of anticipation.

The self-transcendence of the future is a very difficult idea to grasp. Let us begin, then, with an intuitively much more accessible example.

The Self-Transcendence of Prices

The central assumption of the neoclassical theory of the market is that producers and consumers take prices to be given. In the familiar phrase, they are price-takers. Prices, in other words, are assumed to be independent of their behavior, which is analyzed in terms of their willingness to supply and demand the goods that circulate in a given economy. At the same time, however, the formation of prices is explained with reference to the relative proportion of supply and demand in market transactions: the famous "law" of supply and demand. Marxist economists were the first to complain about what they saw as a contradiction in crediting agents with a causal influence over prices while at the same time assuming that the same agents, somehow unaware of their own power, regard the results of their own actions as a species of natural fact—proof, to their way of thinking, of the total alienation of "bourgeois" economics.[3] Neoclassical theorists, for their part, scoffed at the idea that anyone could see a contradiction in what, for them, amounted to a purely mathematical search for a *fixed point*.

The assumption that economic agents take prices to be fixed certainly does not involve a contradiction; but nor does it have the wholly innocent character that economists have long been in the habit of ascribing to it. Historians of science generally agree that what economic theory, the theory of rational choice, and game theory mean by "equilibrium" has nothing to do with what this term originally meant in rational mechanics. Every decision problem involving at least two agents exhibits the phenomenon of specularity, which is to say that each agent is obliged to take into account what he imagines the other thinks he is planning to do, and so on. The economist's type of equilibrium is a way of halting this potentially infinite regress. Neoclassical theory, in assuming that prices are given, makes it clear at exactly which point the regress stops. But economists have never provided a satisfactory justification for this key move. They are content simply to say that agents cannot affect prices to any perceptible degree. This line of argument, doubtful on its face (consumers, for example, can join together to form cooperatives, workers to form unions, and so on), is proof that economists unhesitatingly endorse, perhaps without even knowing it, a metaphysical hypothesis whose plausibility may be challenged. Economists will strenuously object, of course, saying that they do not deal in metaphysical hypotheses. Why? Because economics, they say, is a science. But even if it were to be conceded for the sake of argument that economics may legitimately claim the status of a true science, the fact remains—as Karl Popper long ago demonstrated, irrefutably to my mind—that every science rests on metaphysical foundations. Rather than take refuge in an outmoded positivism, economists, no less than other scientists, will be better advised to frankly acknowledge the metaphysical dimension of their theories, and to explicitly state its implications so that they can be subjected to critical scrutiny.

To say that the system of prices does not depend on the behavior of individual agents means just this: having arrived at a decision, and yet before acting on it, I ask myself what would happen if I were to decide otherwise. In comparing the consequences of what I have decided to do with those that would be entailed by another decision, I hold the system of prices constant, taking them to be fixed. On that assumption there exists only one realized—or, as philosophers say, actual—world, even though two or more worlds are possible. What I compare in order to assure myself that I am making, or have made, the right decision are therefore not two actual worlds, but rather *the* actual world and some number of other possible worlds. The notion that prices are given disguises a deeper claim, namely, that in all these possible worlds, including the world as it actually is, prices are the same.

Allow me to pause for a moment here and ask readers who find the exposition of the argument up to this point elementary, or even superfluous, to bear with me a bit longer. They shall soon see that the implications are nothing short of revolutionary. In comparing an actual world and another possible world we make use of a linguistic and metaphysical device known as a *counterfactual conditional proposition*. A conditional proposition of the "if *p* then *q*" type may be indicative ("If it rains tomorrow, I will not go to work") or counterfactual ("If I were wealthier than I am, I would buy a Lamborghini"). The term "counterfactual" refers here to the presence of an antecedent ("If I were wealthier") that is contrary to fact (alas, I am not wealthier than I am). The truth-status of these two types of conditionals is not at all the same, however. To take a classic example, the proposition "If Shakespeare did not write *Troilus and Cressida*, someone else did" is indubitably true since the play exists, and so it must have an author. By contrast, to assert the truth of the counterfactual proposition "If Shakespeare had not written *Troilus and Cressida*, someone else would have," is highly problematic—at least for those who believe that only the Bard could have produced a masterpiece of this order.

Counterfactual propositions concern possible worlds, worlds that exist somewhere near our world—neighbors, in a sense, of the actual world, which after all is the only one we know firsthand. Nevertheless we cannot do without such propositions in our thinking and reasoning about the past and the future, for example when something important happens that might not have occurred or, conversely, when something does not happen that, if it had occurred, would have changed our life and the world, for better or for worse. Several dozen times during the course of the Cold War our leaders came within a whisker (as it is ritually said) of unleashing a nuclear war that might have made the human race extinct. Could it be that this continual flirting with the inconceivable somehow protected us? Consider the Fukushima catastrophe of March 2011. It might not have occurred had the seawalls built to protect against a tsunami been a few meters higher. If the walls had not been overtopped, the panicked flight from nuclear energy that followed probably would not have taken place, at least not right away. In this virtual world we would not have known how unsafe the civilian nuclear power industry in Japan and elsewhere really is, and so we would have continued walking along the tightrope: the industry's survival depends, after all, on the nonoccurrence of accidents that are considered to be unthinkable before they occur. A thought experiment of this sort shows us that the virtual is indeed a part of reality, in the first place because the free agents who populate the actual world continually ask themselves questions about possible worlds (which therefore seem to them almost to hover over their own); but also because the choices they make depend on the answers they give to these questions.

The answers to counterfactual questions, which is to say questions relating to nearby virtual worlds, necessarily contain an element of indeterminacy. Consider the question "How would the course of human history have been different if Cleopatra's nose had been shorter?" It can be answered in various ways that are neither arbitrary nor wholly determined, ways that variously influence how one thinks about the Roman Empire and what came after. Historians now accept, albeit still with some reluctance, the legitimacy of such a line of inquiry. What would the world be like today if Nazi Germany had built a nuclear bomb before the United States? What if the Soviet Union had won the Cold War? What if Saint Paul had been killed on setting out from Damascus, so that Christianity never became the cornerstone of Western civilization?[4] It will be obvious that no historical science can furnish an unequivocal response to these questions, for they belong as much to the realm of meaning and interpretation as to the realm of cause and effect. One cannot help but suspect that it is because economic theory aspires to the status of what it thinks of as a true science, on a level with the natural sciences, that it has never openly acknowledged the importance of counterfactuals. And yet the whole edifice of economic theory rests on an unspoken assumption—what can only be considered to be a metaphysical postulate. Because this postulate has never been explicitly stated, it has never really been discussed. My purpose in this second chapter is to do just this.

The justification that economists give for assuming that prices are given leads on directly to their implicit theory of counterfactuals. To say that agents take prices to be fixed—external to their behavior and unaffected by it in any possible world—amounts to saying that in deciding which course of action to choose they take prices to be *counterfactually independent* of what they do. Note, however, that the argument economists advance in support of this assumption is that individual agents have no *causal* power over prices; that is, nothing they do can cause prices to change. But this can only count as a reason if from the absence of a causal relation one can deduce the absence of a counterfactual relation. Moreover, the fact that this justification, rather than any other, is invoked as a ground for what, as I say, is the key assumption of standard microeconomic theory suggests that economists are unable to think of counterfactual independence as anything other than the consequence of causal independence.

This view, that counterfactual independence obtains between two variables if and only if causal independence obtains between them, I shall call *the causalist hypothesis*. To put it another way: a variable depends counterfactually on another only if it depends on it causally; and if one variable depends causally on another, then it depends counterfactually on it. In regarding prices as given, economists implicitly take the causalist hypothesis to be true. This is the central metaphysical claim of neoclassical theory. There is nonetheless good reason to doubt it.

That there may be counterfactual dependence even in the absence of causal dependence is attested by many examples that can be interpreted in the same way. It may easily be imagined, for example, even if we have no proof of it, that somewhere today there is a man who missed his flight to New York from Boston on the morning of 11 September 2001. As a psychological matter, it is hardly implausible to suppose that he still trembles at the thought of this happenstance, and that he will tremble from it as long as he lives. Why? Because he says to himself, "If I hadn't missed my plane, I would have died a gruesome death whose circumstances are known to the entire world." What justifies him in this belief, of course, is the causalist hypothesis: whether or not he missed the flight could not have had any causal effect on the unfolding of the tragedy, and therefore no counterfactual effect; accordingly, if he had not missed the flight, the tragedy would have occurred in exactly the same way and he would have been counted among the victims.

I maintain, to the contrary, that this inference is unwarranted. A story from my own personal experience will explain why. It will also show that metaphysics, far from being a cold and abstruse discipline, is often intimately associated with our deepest feelings and emotions. My daughter, who lives and works in Brazil, was on board Air France flight 447 from Rio de Janeiro to Paris on 31 May 2009. Had she delayed her flight by a day she would have been counted among the victims of the horrible accident that followed. At least this is what I said to myself when finally—I was traveling myself at the time—I learned of the catastrophe and heard that my daughter had arrived in Paris safe and sound the day before. Perhaps I was wrong. Seeking to relieve my anxiety, my daughter said to me: "But Dad, if I'd flown the next day the crash wouldn't have occurred!" By that she meant that she had been born under a lucky star: in all the possible worlds in which she might have been on an Air France flight between Rio and Paris, no accident would have occurred. This belief, perfectly rational and yet madly optimistic at the same time, by itself invalidates the causalist hypothesis.

It is therefore not sufficient to assume, as neoclassical theorists believe they are bound to do, that agents have no significant causal influence over prices, in order to justify regarding prices as fixed in advance of actual market transactions—which is to say, as counterfactually independent of agents' decisions. But neither is it necessary to assume this. Agents may be assumed, without the least contradiction, both to have a causal power over prices *and* to take them to be given. We saw earlier that Marxists in the 1960s made a great fuss over this, charging that such agents are "alienated" in the sense that they are prevented from appreciating the true extent of their market power. This need not be true: agents may choose to behave *as if* they were alienated. But why would they do such a thing? Because, as I say, they can coordinate their actions only if they find a way to avoid being trapped in the potentially infinite regress to which they are otherwise condemned by their need to know how much others know of what they know, how much others know of what they know of what others know of what they know, and so on without end. The countervailing need to put a halt to the reflexive action of specularity[5] leads to a shared interest in holding a certain set of variables constant. Agents consciously decide, as a matter of *convention*, to regard these variables as fixed (that is, counterfactually independent of their actions), although they know full well they have a causal power over them. There can be no objection to considering this to be a possible state of affairs. Not only is it perfectly plausible, as a psychological matter, but it supplies an objective basis for developing the concept of a coordination convention, which has slowly but steadily gained acceptance in contemporary economic theory.[6]

This brief metaphysical detour has yielded an essential insight: the assumption on which neoclassical theory rests, that prices are given, cannot be justified by appeal to an unalterable feature of the world, namely, the absence of a causal link between behavior and prices; it is a product instead of convention, which is to say an agreement, if only implicit, freely arrived at by economic agents for the purpose of facilitating exchange. We are dealing, then, not with nature, but with politics.

In order for individual behaviors to be coordinated with one another, the causal power that economic agents as a group have over the determination of prices has to bring about the very set of prices that each agent, in calculating his own personal interest, has taken as a fixed guide to the future. Calculation and causality must therefore be connected in the form of a *loop*. This state of being linked together is what economists call an *equilibrium*. A more unfortunate choice of words can hardly be imagined.[7] The image it calls to mind, of a scale whose two trays support equal weights, obscures what is essentially a circular relation: a continuous loop that has been severed and then reconstituted by joining its two pieces together again at the point where they were separated. This raises two questions, to which economists have given various replies: How is such an operation performed? Who is the surgeon?

The best answer to both of these questions is, or ought to be: the market itself. By virtue of its properties of self-organization and self-transcendence, the market is able to project itself outside of itself and create a more or less large set of points of reference—a system of prices—on which each agent relies in deciding what course of action to adopt. That the neoclassical theory of the market should have found it impossible to free itself from a much simpler schema that involves a genuine, but nevertheless wholly implausible, exteriority is illuminating. Walras imagined that all markets, for commodities and labor alike, function on the model of an auction house. An auctioneer announces a set of prices and then, by a process of gradual adjustment (*tâtonnement*), determines which ones bring supply fully into alignment with demand, actual transactions taking place only once these "equilibrium" prices have been reached and made public. As far as Walras was concerned, of course, this was only of a manner of speaking, a figurative way of picturing how markets work: *as if* they resembled an auction house. Not for a moment did he believe that this primitive thought experiment described how markets *actually* work. It is an unsurpassable irony, then, that the theory of general economic equilibrium in this extremely simplified form—simplified to the point of mutilation, in fact, and almost automatically associated today with libertarian ideologies of one sort or another—should have found its ideal expression in the model known as market socialism. Developed mainly by the Polish economist Oskar Lange, it sought to combine a socialist regime of collective ownership of the means of production with the mode of price calculation associated with general equilibrium theory. Walras's auctioneer became a central planner, in effect, presiding over a mixed regime meant to place economic efficiency in the service of social justice.

I cannot help but think that the political misadventures of general equilibrium theory are due to the fact that it never worked out its own metaphysical implications, particularly with regard to the mechanism of self-transcendence it implicitly assumes. Thus, for example, since market social-ism limited itself to *simulating* the model of general economic equilibrium, it borrowed from this model only the mechanical procedure of calculating prices. We have already seen that it is the feedback effect of causality on calculation that gives prices the power of self-transcendence. But it should be obvious that the simulation of a causal relation by means of a mechanical procedure, or algorithm, is not the same thing as the actual operation of the causal relation itself.[8]

The Self-Transcendence of the Future

Economics, like any self-respecting science, feels obliged to make predictions. But this is not a good idea. Think how often economists are mocked for their mistaken forecasts! It would be unfair to single out this or that individual who set himself up as an oracle and then failed to see a financial catastrophe rising in the distance like a tidal wave. Besides, there are too many examples to choose from. Economists who venture to say what the rate of GDP growth or the rate of inflation will be tomorrow find themselves in a radically dif-ferent position with regard to future events than researchers in the physical sciences. The predictions made by physicists or astronomers do not affect the behavior of the boson or the supernova they are studying. It is a quite dif-ferent matter, however, when a prominent economist, or a politician posing as an economist, makes a public statement forecasting the movement of a key financial variable. If economic agents take these false prophets at their word, as they are apt to do in the hope of advancing their own individual self-interest, there is a very good chance their behavior will bring about a state of the world different from the one that was predicted.

A good prediction ought therefore to take into account the impact it is likely to have on the world. Imagine a person who has reason to believe that his reputation as a preeminent authority on some subject will lead other people to believe what he says about the future is true and calculate their own interest accordingly. In planning ahead, in other words, people will take the future as he has foretold it to be *settled* or *determined*; more precisely, in considering the various courses of action open to them they hold the predicted contours of the future constant in their deliberations. This, at least, is what the forecaster believes will happen, and, as I say, he has good reasons for believing it.

The question arises, however, whether the forecaster, in causing agents to suppose that the future is fixed in this sense, deprives them of their free will. Surely he must see that, precisely because they are endowed with free will, they *can* change the future. A familiar expression, "change the future"— but what exactly does it mean? In our ordinary, everyday metaphysics, as it might be called, we are incapable of doing any such thing: the future is no less inalterable than the past. It is not true, in other words, that the future can be any different today than it will be. Nothing that I do between now and any particular moment in the future can justify me in believing that *if I do this, the future will be different* (indicative conditional proposition). David K. Lewis expressed this idea in the following terms, in which the mood and tense of the verbs have a crucial importance:

> What we *can* do by way of "changing the future" (so to speak) is to bring it about that the future is the way it actually will be, rather than any of the other ways it would have been if we acted differently in the present. That is something like change. We make a difference. But it is not literally change, since the difference we make is between actuality and other possibilities, *not between successive actualities.* The literal truth is just that *the future depends counterfactually on the present.* It depends, partly, on what we do now."[9]

It is just this counterfactual dependence that agents are deprived of when they believe our hypothetical forecaster. Plainly he cannot deny that they have a causal power over the future. He therefore ascribes to them the ability to violate the causalist hypothesis. Agents, in his view, have a causal power over the future while at the same time holding the future to be counterfactually independent of their actions. It is on this basis that the forecaster reckons how the future will turn out, by taking into account the effects of his prediction, which has become a fixed point of reference in the calculations that the agents themselves make about the future. Here we find the same loop we encountered in the previous section with regard to the self-transcendence of prices.

What is the nature of prediction in this model? Clearly it is not the same thing as divination: no message reaches the forecaster from the future, having already been written down on the great scroll of universal history; the irreversibility of time is an ineliminable fact of the world. Nor is prediction the same thing as what philosophers call voluntarism (or decisionism): the forecaster does not impose on his listeners a future that, for reasons known only to him, he finds suitable; he cannot reconnect the severed ends of the loop without taking the reaction of agents into account. Neither fatalism nor voluntarism, this particular relationship to the future has its own logic and its own metaphysics.

It would be a grave error, by the way, to suppose that we are dealing here with one of those pointless thought experiments that have always fascinated philosophers, from Plato's allegory of the cave to the brain-in-a-vat puzzles that arouse such enthusiasm today. The problem I have in mind goes back to before Plato's time, and in one or another version has had a considerable impact on human affairs throughout the ages. Biblical prophecy and the theory of the market are the alpha and the omega of these various incarnations.

The prophets of the Bible were extraordinary figures, often great eccentrics. Whatever else may be said of them, they did not go unnoticed by their neighbors. There can be no doubt that the influence their prophecies had on the world around them and on the course of events had purely human and social causes; but it was due also to the fact that those who heard them believed that the word of the prophet was the word of the Lord and that this word, which came to the prophet directly, from on high, had the power to bring about the very thing that it announced. We would say today that the word of the prophet had a *performative* power: in saying things, he brought them into being. Mind you, the prophet was well aware of this. One might be tempted to conclude that the prophet had the power to which political revolutionaries aspire: he spoke so that things might change in the direction that he wished to impress upon them. But this would be to overlook the fatalistic aspect of prophecy, which reads out the names of all those things that will come to pass, just as they are written down on the great scroll of history, immutably, ineluctably. Thus Jeremiah (13:23): "Can the Ethiopian change his skin or the leopard his spots? Then may you also do good who are accustomed to do evil." Evildoers, the biblical prophet says, are doomed forever to do evil.

Revolutionary prophecy, particularly in the form it came to acquire in Marxist doctrine, has preserved the highly paradoxical mixture of fatalism and voluntarism that characterizes biblical prophecy. "Here," Hans Jonas observes in connection with Marxism, moving from the same metaphysical point of departure that I have chosen, "we have world-historical prognosis on a rational basis—and at the same time, through the unique equation of what must be with what ought to be, a goal-setting for the political *will*, which is thereby itself made a factor in proving the theory true after the latter's pre-affirmed truth had first motivated the will on its part. For the political action thus determined, which makes happen what must happen, this closed circuit creates *a most peculiar mixture of colossal responsibility for the future with deterministic release from responsibility.*"[10]

Biblical prophecy is included in its own discourse, one might say, for it sees itself as bringing about the very event that it announces as destiny. Its self-referentiality, in other words, is conscious. The prophet is searching for the *fixed point* of the future, the point at which human volition achieves the very thing that fate dictates. There are nevertheless situations where no fixed point exists. This is the metaphysical trap into which the prophet Jonah fell: he knew that his prophecy, in acting upon the world (and by virtue of the very fact of its acting upon the world), would turn out to be false. How, then, could he not have resented his treatment at the hands of the Lord, who had ensnared him in the labyrinth we call time?

When the prophet identifies the future with a fixed point of the loop connecting the future that has been predicted and the future that has been causally realized—which is to say with an image, or conception, of the world whose prediction produces a world conforming to it—this very future is brought into existence, actualized, and everyone can see that the prophet was speaking the truth. Note, however, that he was speaking the truth not because the future was unveiled to him in the form of a miraculous apparition, but because he had *calculated* what would happen by taking into account the repercussions of his forecast.

Modern sociological theory, and later economic theory, popularized the notion of a self-fulfilling prophecy: a statement concerning the future that has the appearance of being true, not because it was true to begin with, but because it causes those who hear or read it to react in ways that, taken together, make it true, or at least congruent with what will come to pass.[11] The recent global financial crisis gave this idea a notoriety it did not previously have. The classic example of a self-fulfilling prophecy in economic life is regularly witnessed when agents anticipate that prices will rise by a certain amount and plan accordingly, with the result that a rise in prices equal to the one that was anticipated actually occurs. It is tempting to suppose that prophecy in the sense that I have in mind is merely one of the forms assumed by self-fulfilling prophecy. But that would be to miss a crucial aspect of reflexivity in this instance. The prophet whose situation I am trying to describe knows everything that I have just said when he utters his prophecy: he anticipates the future *in the knowledge that* that it will assume the form of a self-fulfilling prophecy. The logic of self-fulfilling prophecy can easily be accounted for within the framework of traditional metaphysics. It is the additional element of reflexivity introduced by the prophet's own lucidity, by his own awareness of how the future he foretells will come about, that tips us over into a whole other metaphysics of temporality.

Public Speech in a Time of Financial Panic

To read or listen to commentary on the financial crisis in the years since 2007, one might have the impression that the model of self-transcendence I have just described has become rather familiar by now, even if no one knows it by this name. But in fact confusion on this point is widespread, and scarcely less troubling than the misapprehensions that stifle clear thinking about market self-regulation. Troubling, not least, because it is yet another sign of the bewildering of politics by economics—what might be called *economystification*.

Public figures say they often face a dilemma: should they tell people the truth when news is bad and there is a danger of frightening the markets, and so of bringing about the very catastrophe they seek to avoid—the danger of the self-fulfilling prophecy[12]—or should they keep quiet instead, at the risk of appearing afterward to have been either incompetent or self-serving? Even if they do keep quiet, will they not just as surely bring about the catastrophe, since silence will be suspected of concealing some terrible reality?[13] Clearly this way of posing the question suffers from a fatal contradiction: on the one hand, leaders believe that public speech, insofar as it succeeds in being prophetic, has an impact on the future; on the other, they continue to act as if reality is independent of the way in which it is thought and spoken of— as if they believe that recognizing the existence of a certain state of affairs would not make any difference, since things are the way they are and nothing anyone can do will change that. It is remarkable that this second proposition, which was abandoned long ago in the natural sciences, should still be accepted as part of what is imagined to be a scientific approach to the study of human affairs.

What separates the prophet from everyone else, or so it would appear at first sight, is that he stands apart from the phenomenon of specularity. His words are supposed to tell the truth—the truth about the future, which is taken by agents as a fixed element for purposes of analysis and planning. In reality, of course, the prophet, in the sense in which I intend the term, stands so little apart from the obsessive regard agents have for one other that he deliberately causes it to enter into their calculations, so that the predicted future and the actual future will coincide. And yet one may wonder whether the best prophet, from an agent's point of view, is not someone one who does *not* take into account the effect of his words on his listeners; someone who simply knows or divines what the future will be. In other words, an expert.

It will be helpful to distinguish three ways of piercing the veil of the future: prediction, futurism, and prophecy. At one extreme is the predictor, or forecaster, who stands in the same relation to the human and social system he studies as someone who seeks to predict the evolution of a particular dynamic system in the natural world: he constructs a mathematical model of the system and either solves the equations analytically or runs a computer program. There is no difference whatever, so far as method is concerned, between predicting the future of Chinese energy consumption and calculating the trajectory of a space probe. At the other extreme, where free will is given its greatest rein, stands the futurist. The futurist disavows any ambition of forming a coherent body of knowledge about the future on the ground that (in the philosopher Gaston Berger's phrase) one doesn't predict the future, one builds it. In that case one limits oneself to exploring a set of "possible futures"[14]—to devising a series of alternate scenarios, marking out a "thousand paths of the future"[15]—while leaving the task of choosing among them to the political authorities. Whereas a person who seeks to predict the future places too much faith in a deterministic science, the futurist places too much faith in human free will. The attitude of the prophet, as we have seen, lies somewhere between these two extremes.

The expert, the one who knows, is the forecaster whom I just mentioned. Why would economic agents prefer to deal with an expert rather than a prophet? The main thing from their point of view, as I say, is to be able to coordinate their behavior with reference to a conception of the future that is a matter of common knowledge, in the technical sense that this phrase has acquired in philosophy.[16] Paradoxically, the expert, who is content to know without having to think about what he knows—about its origins, its truth-conditions, its impact on reality—may often seem to be a more reliable guide than the prophet, whom agents are inclined to suspect of thinking too much. This paradox needs to be carefully considered.

Not hundreds of thousands, but now, with the advent of globalization, hundreds of millions of economic agents—everybody, you and I no less than the heads of Goldman Sachs and Apple—must be able to coordinate their decision making without having at each moment to stop and ask themselves what everyone else thinks about someone's expectations regarding their behavior, and so on in a potentially infinite sequence. The unlimited specularity needed to satisfy a constant preoccupation of this sort would soon drive all parties completely mad. The market is a social institution that resolves this problem in the most elegant possible way. Each agent relies, not directly on the opinion of others, but on what might be called (to borrow a very ugly piece of jargon from systems theory) interface variables. These variables do away with the need to think about what others think, for they are simultaneously taken by all agents as fixed points of reference—that is, as counterfactually independent of their actions—even though, as they well know, these variables are a synergistic consequence of their own behavior. We have so far considered two major types of interface variable: prices and the future. It now becomes clear that *the market uses the future to achieve coordination*: it projects itself forward by means of a virtual traction point that comes into existence only in, and as a result of, the very same forward movement—a miraculous feat worthy of Baron Münchausen himself.

It now becomes clear, too, why the expert should be not merely a useful, but indeed an indispensable figure. "The expert is a man who has stopped thinking—he knows!," as the architect Frank Lloyd Wright is famously supposed to have said. The markets seldom ask for anything more. In order to function, in order to organize a vast web of interlocking transactions from one day to the next, they need a universally shared conception of the future. It hardly matters whether this conception has any basis in truth. Consider, for example, what the economist André Orléan called the Reagan effect.[17] One day, in December 1987, President Reagan made it known that in his opinion the dollar had fallen too far. It must appreciate in value, he declared; it will appreciate, he predicted. No currency dealer attached the least credit to the president's judgment of such matters. This was the same man, after all, who blamed the dollar's decline on the excessively low interest rates engineered by America's competitors—a far-fetched explanation, to say the least, since the higher the rate of interest a currency commands, the more attractive it is to buyers and the higher its price. Even so, the majority of foreign exchange traders bought dollars on hearing the news. Was this irrational? No, because they anticipated that other traders would do the same, driving up the price of the dollar. And so it came to pass.

The "expert" prediction came true in this case, but more often than not it is subsequently proved to be false. Events contradict the confident assurances of even the most reputable authorities with surprising regularity.[18] The markets seldom concern themselves with the trustworthiness of the experts who make such predictions, however, for there what matters above everything else is not being mistaken about the expectations of other market participants. The prophet finds himself in an altogether different situation. In the biblical understanding, as we know from Deuteronomy, the sole criterion of a true prophet's knowledge is that his words come true—that his prophecy proves to be accurate: "And if you say in your heart, 'How shall we know the word which the Lord has not spoken?'—when a prophet speaks in the name of the Lord, *if the thing does not happen or come to pass, that is the thing the Lord has not spoken*; the prophet has spoken it presumptuously; you shall not be afraid of him."[19] In other words, the nonrealization of a prophecy proves that it is not of divine origin. Only the future can decide. The expert, by contrast, is not subject to this constraint: he can say whatever he likes; what matters to traders in a market is that each of them can count on the others to take the expert's words as a fixed point of reference in their calculations, so that it becomes a matter of common knowledge in the strict sense of the term.

The inherent myopia of expertise makes it liable from time to time to tragically stupid errors of judgment. One thinks of credit-rating agencies in particular. By making public their evaluation of a bank's or a country's present position, they give the future no other choice than to raise the bidding on past tendencies. The power and influence conferred by recent legislation[20] on a handful of experts who have already more than once displayed their incompetence have created a situation in which an unfavorable rating plunges the bank or country in question into a downward spiral from which it will have the greatest trouble extricating itself. American institutional investors, in particular, are required by law to withdraw their funds under such circumstances, making it almost inevitable that the economy of a country such as Greece will spin out of control. The rating agencies protest: we are the thermometer, not the disease—as if the public disclosure of the patient's temperature will have no impact on the development of his illness! Some accuse the agencies of having usurped the function of an oracle. But an oracle, no less than a prophet, has to take into account the impact of its pronouncement on the course of events in order to accurately foretell them. Any action performed with the purpose of foiling a tragic prophecy has a causal effect on the likelihood of its being fulfilled or not. The oracle has foreseen all such actions, however. This is why it always turns out to be right. One cannot help but be reminded of *the force of destiny* that irrevocably brings misfortune upon Oedipus. Under pretense of objectivity and neutrality, the rating agencies behave like apprentice sorcerers. Even when the future seems to confirm their pessimism, because publicizing a rating downgrade causes it to be justified by events, they maintain that they have simply judged the situation correctly and that their opinion had no effect on the final outcome. This is the stupidity of expertise.

The surest sign that Economy has succeeded in subjugating politics is that a chief of state is now expected to be an expert in economics. The greater his presumed expertise, the greater his chances of being elected or appointed. Already economists have been elevated to the highest office of their lands. But a chief of state who thinks and behaves like an economist can only be a wicked politician.

Communication in an Age of Catastrophe

A growing number of scientific authorities tell us that catastrophic weather events are inevitable if we do not drastically change our course of economic development. As a theoretical and practical matter both, we face an alarming dilemma. On the one hand, experts assure us that the world's climate is indeed warming, that this warming is due in the main to human activity, and that its local and global effects will be disastrous. On the other hand, the same experts confess that their predictions are subject to a very substantial margin of error. They cannot say, for example, whether by the year 2100 the average global temperature will have risen by 1.1 or by 6.4 degrees Celsius—a difference of some 9.5 degrees Fahrenheit![21]

Among laymen, who include members of the political class as well as decision makers in the broad sense, this counterbalancing of certainty by uncertainty produces quite different reactions, ranging from panic to indifference. For all those, such as myself, who are convinced that the situation is grave and that there is no alternative but to act at once, a question arises as to the logical status that should be granted to the uncertainty of predictions, and—a separate question—how this uncertainty should be explained to the public. A great deal of confusion would be avoided, it seems to me, if the idea of self-transcendence were to be kept in mind.

When scientists and engineers address the question of risks, they may be counted on to draw a distinction between "objective" risks, which can be more or less precisely measured, and "perceived" or "subjective" risks, which typically are associated with poorly informed, if not actually irrational individuals. Science imagines itself to be under an obligation to inform and educate the public in such a way that perceived risks are brought as closely as possible into alignment with objective risks—which, of course, are supposed to be the only real risks there are. This is a false distinction, however, for it grows out of a deep philosophical confusion between what is subjective and what is agent-relative. The risks perceived by an ordinary person are not necessarily less objective than the ones perceived by a scientist. Whatever difference there may be between their assessments can be explained by a perfectly objective circumstance, namely, the place of the observer in relation to the risk. Consider two limiting cases, one in which the observer observes an action performed by someone else, the other in which the observer and the agent are the same person (for example, the driver of a vehicle): their perception of risk will diverge for good reasons having nothing to do with any irrationality on the part of the observer-agent.

The Intergovernmental Panel on Climate Change (IPCC) has wrongly been accused by critics of failing to lay sufficient emphasis on the uncertainty that hampers its forecasts. To the contrary, the IPCC has never sought to conceal this striking detail: half of the uncertainty regarding the rise in temperature by 2100—that is, the discrepancy between 1.1°C and 6.4°C—derives from the uncertainty over the level of global greenhouse-gas emissions a few dozen years from now, which depends in turn on uncertainty about whether governments will act aggressively to deal with the problem or adopt more or less noninterventionist policies. Moral and psychological elements therefore play a decisive role in determining the scale of the uncertainty associated with changes in the climate system. Plainly this uncertainty is not at all subjective. To think of the climate system and, more generally, all those ecosystems in which mankind is both observer and actor as if they were dynamic physical systems, and nothing more, would be a gross oversimplification. It is this special kind of complexity that makes attempts to predict the exact course of global warming over the next century both difficult and perilous. But prediction is not what researchers at the IPCC and elsewhere do. Instead they draw up scenarios, in the tradition of Jouvenel and the early futurists. But this, I am convinced, is no longer enough: only by adopting the methods of prophecy—in the technical and wholly secular sense that I have given this practice—will it be possible to escape catastrophe. It is of the highest importance that we try to understand why.

No sensible person disputes that human activity has an influence on the climate; indeed, as we now know, climate change is in large part the result of human activity. Decisions that are now being taken, or will soon be taken, promise to have a crucial impact on the evolution of the global climate system: if humanity resolves to limit its emissions of greenhouse gases, major catastrophes may possibly be avoided; if not, they unquestionably will occur. A group like the IPCC would have no reason to exist if matters were otherwise. The reason so many scientists are now studying the causes of climate change is not simply that they are attracted by challenging scientific problems. It is mainly that they aspire to exert an influence on the decision making of politicians and, in a larger sense, of the people whom politicians represent. Scientists see themselves as experts in a position to modify, if not the climate itself, then at least the climate of opinion.

As obvious as all this may seem, none of it is taken into account when it comes to making projections. Policies aimed at reducing greenhouse-gas emissions are, of course, represented in mathematical models, but only in the form of control variables or parameters, as though human behavior were an independent (or, as economists say, "exogenous") variable. The value of this variable determines which particular scenario is selected from a set of possible futures. Enforcing a rigid distinction between what is taken to be objective (the physical system) and what is taken to be subjective (a set of human decisions, the product to one degree or another of free will) is a serious error, on both methodological and philosophical grounds, for it leaves out an essential element: the decisions that are made, or not made, themselves depend in part on publicly announced expectations of the future, and the future itself depends on which decisions are made and which ones are not. This causal loop is both a cause and a consequence of the fact that human knowledge, including that part of it which bears on the future, is indissociable from human behavior. It is this loop that prohibits us from treating human behavior as an independent variable.

The debate over the manner in which the IPCC operates involves important (though, for our purposes here, incidental) questions, such as the honesty of experts, their reluctance or inability to communicate technical findings that can be fully understood only in the context of information to which the public does not have access, and so forth. But the really fundamental issue—self-transcendence, which is to say the feedback of the causal effects of predicting the future upon the future itself—is never mentioned. If the future causally depends on the way in which it is anticipated, and this anticipation is made public using a certain kind of language and a certain mode of description, any attempt to shape the future must take this element of anticipation into account, as well as the manner in which it is received by both private citizens and government officials and the manner in which they act in response to it. *The way the future is described and understood is part of what determines the future.* Or, as a philosopher might say, the reciprocal linkage between the epistemological and the ontological is an objective feature of human affairs. This fact suggests a criterion for any adequate description of the future: the future under such a description must be a fixed point of the loop connecting past and future that is characteristic of prophetic utterances.

Psychology—in the event, cognitive psychology—has something to contribute to this analysis, though without lessening or detracting in any way from its objective character. Cognitive psychologists note that our idea of rationality includes the principle that choices ought not depend on the contingent, and sometimes arbitrary, ways in which they are described—or "framed," as they say. A spectacular series of experiments conducted more than thirty years ago by Daniel Kahneman and the late Amos Tversky showed that the ordering of subjects' preferences depends on whether a decision problem is presented in one form rather than another. I summarize one of these experiments here, for it exposes a sophism that is often encountered in discussing the relation between economics and ecology. Subjects are presented successively with three problems:

PROBLEM 1: Which of the following options do you prefer?
  A. A sure win of $30 [78%]
  B. An 80% chance to win $45 [22%]

PROBLEM 2: Consider the following two-stage game. In the first stage there is a 75% chance to end the game without winning anything, and a 25% chance to move into the second stage. If you reach the second stage you have a choice between:
  C. A sure win of $30 [74%]
  D. An 80% chance to win $45 [26%]
Your choice must be made before the game starts (i.e., before the outcome of the first stage is known). Please indicate the option you prefer.

PROBLEM 3: Which of the following options do you prefer?
    E. A 25% chance to win $30 [42%]
    F. A 20% chance to win $45 [58%][22]

It will readily be seen that these three problems are logically equivalent. Problems 2 and 3 are arithmetically identical. As for problems 1 and 2, they are identical if the second stage is reached for problem 2; and the fact of choosing option C or D in no way changes the outcome if the game stops after the first step. But whereas the subjects answered similarly to the first two problems, their response to the third was very different.

The difference in the responses to problems 1 and 3 illustrates the famous Allais paradox. Maurice Allais, a future Nobel laureate in economics, demonstrated in 1953 that the preferences of many subjects (including some of the top decision theorists of the period) systematically violated the axioms of the mathematical theory of expected utility.[23] In particular, he showed that reducing the absolute assurance of winning by a given proportion—here a reduction of 20%, from 100% to 80%—has much greater psychological weight than a similar reduction in the middle range of probabilities—in this case from 25% to 20%. Certainty, in other words, is prized and desired for its own sake. Because subjects are prepared to pay any price in order to be sure of winning, they strongly prefer option A to option B in the first problem, even though the latter option promises a higher expected utility ($36, or 80% of $45, rather than $30), whereas a majority prefers option F to option E in the third problem. Tversky and Kahneman call this the "certainty effect."

And yet the most troubling thing here is the difference in response to problems 2 and 3, which once again are arithmetically identical. The only explanation is that the subjects treat problem 2 as they treated problem 1, which is to say as a function of the certainty effect. And yet there is no certainty involved in problem 2; or, rather, the certainty is simply an illusion, due to the way in which the problem is framed, having arbitrarily been divided into two stages. Tversky and Kahneman speak here of a "pseudocertainty effect" and elsewhere, oxymoronically, of "contingent certainty."[24]

Taken together, this set of problems brings out in a very subtle fashion the essential role played by contingently certain outcomes in negotiation, but also, more generally, in all cases where interests or values come into conflict. Tversky and Kahneman gave the following example, suggested perhaps by their personal experience as officers in the Israeli Defense Forces. They ask us to imagine the political debate in a democratic country, surrounded by hostile neighbors, that contemplates giving up occupied foreign territories. In the event of war, these territories represent a strategic asset that would undoubtedly contribute to victory. On the other hand, handing over these territories would lessen the probability of war, though in a way that remains fundamentally uncertain. It is likely, they conclude, that the party in favor of continuing to occupy the territories will prevail, owing to the perceived superiority of the contingent certainty over mere probability.[25] In effect, then, one is ready to choose C, though not E.

The dilemmas posed by industrial and technological development present many analogous situations. The most obvious example is the way in which the choice between economic growth and ecology is framed in developed countries, particularly with regard to the question of climate change. The dominant school of opinion holds that under no circumstances should economic growth be sacrificed for the sake of protecting the environment: in the event that the prospect of catastrophe becomes more likely, a strong economy and advanced technologies will be invaluable assets in moving promptly and effectively to confront it. This pseudocertainty effect is bound to win out over the argument that continued growth increases the probability of a major ecological crisis.

Is there any way to demystify the pseudocertainty effect, so that contingent certainty is seen for what it is, a pure illusion? That would amount, mathematically speaking, to framing decisions in every possible case under the third rather than the second formulation. But then one runs up against another cognitive obstacle: most people are unused to dealing with probabilities lying in the range between zero and one, and prefer to reason in terms of two basic modal categories, certainty and impossibility.

A well-known experiment performed by the cognitive psychologists Leda Cosmides and John Tooby beautifully illustrates this point.[26] A group of subjects that included physicians was given to consider a disease that, on average, affects one person in a thousand. There is a test for detecting it, they were told, but it has a false positive rate of 5%. Imagine the result of the test in your case is positive. What would you reckon the probability of your having the disease to be? The overwhelming majority of subjects, physicians included, said 95%. The correct answer is 2%, as a classical Bayesian analysis demonstrates. The surprising thing is that one has only to describe the problem in terms of frequencies, rather than of probabilities, for the correct answer to leap to the eyes of most subjects. Out of a thousand persons tested, one on average will have the disease. The test will be positive for this person (assuming there are no false negatives), but it will also be positive for 50 other persons. Only one out of fifty-one who test positive will really have the disease, then, or just shy of 2%. The human mind, as Cosmides and Tooby put it, is a machine for making frequentist inferences. But it is very poorly equipped for reasoning about singular events, which by their nature are unique, such as a major ecological catastrophe. As a consequence, people find it very difficult to avoid traps set by the pseudocertainty effect.

The future of the earth's climate, and therefore our future as terrestrial beings, depends at least as much on collective cognitive mechanisms for forming beliefs as on physicochemical laws that govern hydrological phenomena and the behavior of the upper atmosphere. But it is the very *objectivity* of these mechanisms, very probably "hardwired" to one degree or another in our brains, that accounts for their force. The journalist Éric le Boucher created a stir some years ago in France when he wrote the following in an article with the deliberately provocative title "The Kyoto Protocol Is on Its Last Legs—Let's Finish It Off!":

> The environmentalists have made a taboo of Kyoto. They are not necessarily wrong to denounce delaying tactics; putting off the effort [to ratify the protocol] until tomorrow may well be unwise. But they ought to understand that they are wrong in believing that they have managed, through [the issue of] climate, to commit the world to another model of development. This is an illusion.
>
> An illusion for the third world, which demands the right to consume. An illusion for the wealthy countries, which refuse to return to the past. Ecology cannot be defined in opposition to the economy; the environment cannot be protected at the expense of development. An ecology wedded to apocalyptic visions of the earth's future will always lose in the end. The only solution to the damage caused by progress is progress.[27]

Evidently Le Boucher had fallen victim to the pseudocertainty effect, no less than the administration of George W. Bush, whose talking points he did nothing more than repeat. No one will be surprised to learn that I consider this approach to be irresponsible. The point I wish to make here is that, before condemning it, we need to fully appreciate the force of the objective mechanisms that combine to give it the appearance of legitimacy.

What is at issue, once again, are the competing claims of expertise and prophecy in human affairs. An expert possesses the truth in a particular domain (in this case, climate science). The problem, he believes, is how to transmit the truth to the rest of society. This is a problem of "communication." The prophet, for his part, believes that there is no truth independent of the way in which it is transmitted. For him, the objectivity of cognitive mechanisms or of crowd phenomena is no less important than the objectivity of climate science. The fault of the IPCC—if in fact it is at fault—lies in its failure to decide between these two attitudes.

Self-Transcendence without Words

The capacity of markets to create self-transcendence does not necessarily involve the speech of a prophet or, in a degraded version, that of an expert. We have shown this to be true in the case of prices: they are formed spontaneously, which is to say mechanically, and serve as a guide for economic agents, without any need of Walras's auctioneer or Lange's central planning board. The same thing may be said with regard to the self-transcendence of the future. It sometimes happens that the course of events indicates a direction all by itself, with such unarguable authority that no one has to speak with anyone else in order to be convinced that what is manifested in this way is the direction of history. This implies, of course, that the general awareness that this direction is the result of self-transcendence is set aside, so to speak. The direction is a fixed point of the process by which the individual reactions of a multitude of persons, each one observing this direction, jointly serve to create it.

One property of market phenomena—a property that has profoundly impressed the greatest economists, regardless of political temperament, from Adam Smith to John Maynard Keynes and Friedrich Hayek, without at all disturbing the deepest convictions of the average economist—is especially important in this connection: imitation. Economy is the domain in which what René Girard calls mimetic desire has been given a free hand.[28] The role played by mimetic desire has been made obvious to us by the world of fashion, and sharpened by our daily experience of advertising. But it is no less evident in the world of business, where, in utter contrast to intellectual and academic life, one makes no secret of one's interest in imitating a rival. More subtly, however, it is also the rule, as Keynes well understood, under conditions of radical uncertainty. In that case the calculation of probabilities is of no help, and the best one can do is to imitate one's neighbors. If you should happen to possess a relevant piece of information that is unknown to me, by following what you do I stand to benefit indirectly from your knowledge. It may be, of course, that you are as much in the dark as I am, but even of this I cannot be at all sure.

Mimetic dynamics have fundamentally different properties from the ones (illicitly borrowed, as we have seen, from rational mechanics and thermodynamics) that economists consider alone worth studying, most prominently in connection with the so-called law of supply and demand. In the wonderfully harmonious universe of neoclassical theory, a departure from equilibrium sets in motion forces that lead the system back to it, like a pendulum that has been deflected from its downward vertical position or a spring that has been compressed. An increase in demand for a good causes its price to rise, discouraging consumers from buying as much of it as they would like and encouraging producers to make more of it, until supply and demand are brought back into balance. Mimetic dynamics, by contrast, amplify sudden swings and generate unforeseen trajectories.

It will be useful at this point to introduce an important conceptual distinction, first made by neocybernetic theories of self-organization in connection with the role of chance in bringing about the emergence of complex systems without appeal to a maker or designer, between two morphogenetic principles: *order from noise* and *complexity from noise*.[29] The difference between these principles may be grasped by considering a pair of experiments requiring only an elementary knowledge of mathematics.

The first is a physical experiment that has been conducted every day by visitors to the Palais de la Découverte in Paris since its opening in 1937. Pressing a button causes a needle to be dropped at random onto a metallic surface that is divided into vertical strips by equidistant parallel lines. The length of the needle is half the distance separating any two neighboring lines.

There are two possible outcomes: either the needle falls across one of the lines that make up the grid, or it does not. A counter continuously updates the number of needles that intersect a line at any moment, expressed as a proportion of the total number of needles dropped onto the surface. Over the last seventy-five years, millions of people have pressed the button. The effect has been to progressively damp oscillations in the value of this proportion, which now approaches ever more closely a limit that is known today with a precision extending to several thousand decimal places. The beginning of it is 0.318309886183791. It happens that the value of this convergent series is the inverse of π (pi)—the relation of the circumference of a circle to its diameter. This means that the value of π itself can be determined experimentally as precisely as one likes. The same experiment has been conducted in a number of other science museums elsewhere in the world, and in all of them the proportion converges on this same value, the inverse of π.

This experiment is known as Buffon's needle, after the great French naturalist Georges-Louis Leclerc, comte de Buffon, who was also an eminent mathematician.[30] It does no more than help us visualize, albeit in a most memorable fashion, the law of large numbers: the frequency of a random event tends over time to approach its a priori probability. In using the methods of the calculus to show that the probability of the needle falling across a line is precisely the inverse of π, Buffon very elegantly demonstrated that chance—"noise," in the jargon of statisticians—is merely the servant of a preexisting necessity: order arises from noise.

The second experiment is a thought experiment that illustrates the morphogenetic power of imitation. Known as Pólya's urn,[31] it has generated a considerable variety of mathematical models. Imagine an urn containing two balls, one white and the other black. A ball is drawn at random, and then put back in the urn along with a new ball of the same color. The number of balls in the urn therefore increases by one with each drawing. What one wants to examine in this case is how the proportion of white balls changes over time. It is a simple matter to simulate this variable distribution using a pocket calculator equipped with a random number generator. One discovers that the dynamic of this very simple system—which nevertheless has a memory built into it—behaves as in the case of Buffon's needle: the oscillations are progressively damped and soon converge on a certain value, which may be obtained with a precision as great as one likes if the experiment is repeated long enough. Surprisingly, this value turns out *not* to be ½. Why is it a surprise? The results of successive drawings are perfectly symmetrical, but eventually the symmetry is broken. What could cause this to happen? There seems to be no rational explanation.

Pólya's urn is the simplest formalization of a mimetic dynamic: each random event—here, the drawing of a ball of a certain color—changes the conditions of the next drawing by modifying the a priori probabilities, strengthening the chances that the color in question will be drawn again. This process of self-reinforcement is nicely illustrated by the story of two absent-minded friends who set out walking together with a particular destination in mind. Neither one actually knows how to get there, but each one believes the other knows. Each one therefore follows the other. The path that results from the two of them imitating each other exhibits a certain stability for a time. But it cannot last, since sooner or later each one will realize his mistake.

Pólya's urn differs from Buffon's needle in one essential respect: with each fresh trial, a *new and different* value emerges as a causal result of the drawing itself. If one looks at individual instances alone, it is impossible to tell the mimetic dynamic apart from the one that characterizes Buffon's needle: in both cases one observes a *convergence* toward a value. And yet looking at a series of drawings from the outside, as it were—a point of view that can be attained only by projecting oneself beyond the individual instance, which now stands revealed as the realization of one among an infinite number of possibilities—one observes an apparently maximal *divergence*: the a priori probability distribution of convergence values is uniform over the set of real numbers in the interval [0,1]. Here we are faced with the phenomenon of complexity from noise, where chance causes a type of necessity to emerge that can be detected only in retrospect, looking back on a series of outcomes.

The relation between a mimetic dynamic and its asymptotic behavior over time (that is, as time approaches infinity) may be pictured as a loop connecting the level of emergent behavior (known as an *attractor*) with the level of the dynamic itself (figure 1).

In complexity from noise, in other words, the dynamic converges toward an attractor generated by the dynamic itself. This sort of evolutionary process is said to be "path-dependent." Here once again we encounter the familiar structure of self-transcendence with its signature loop. The mimetic dynamic seems to be guided by an end that preexists it; indeed, this is how it is

Figure 1. Complexity from Noise

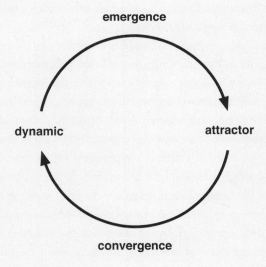

experienced from within. But it is the dynamic itself that brings its own end
into existence. The causality represented by the bottom arrow, which the end
of the path appears to exert on the path itself, is, of course, an illusion: the
future cannot *causally* modify the past. In the universe of materialist causality, there is only the path and nothing else. The path leads onward, always
onward, from one point to the next. In the universe of meaning, by contrast,
and even in the absence of prophetic speech that expresses it in linguistic
form, the direction in which the mimetic dynamic seems to point itself
affects the evolution of the dynamic.

Self-transcendence without prophetic speech is strikingly illustrated by
panic behavior in general, and in particular by market panic, though it cannot
be reduced to such cases.[32] When the crowd loses its leader (in Freud's famous
definition of panic),[33] another guiding force emerges to take his place—the
crowd itself. It is as though the crowd detaches itself from itself, from the
individual persons who make it up, and acquires a kind of autonomy in relation to them, without, however, ceasing to be merely the composite result of
individual actions and reactions. Panic, in other words, is a system effect. Its

self-transcendence cuts off the potentially infinite regress of normal specular behavior, in which each person wonders what every other thinks about him. Everyone looks in a single direction: the one in which panic has caused them to flee. As Durkheim astutely remarked, a crowd or social group caught up in the fervor (or "effervescence") of such moments exhibits all the traits that are customarily ascribed to a divinity: exteriority, transcendence, unpredictability, inaccessibility.[34] Elias Canetti, in his influential work on crowds and power, stressed that "the crowd needs a direction, . . . [a] goal [that is] outside the individual members and common to all of them." The precise nature of the goal does not matter, so long as it is unattained.[35] This is exactly the experience of people who flee in panic—a shared sense of collective identity that the act of flight brings about, all by itself.

No one will deny the market's capacity for self-organization. Like any complex organism, it accomplishes this through a process of self-transcendence, even when it courts disaster. It may well be necessary to regulate markets—to restrain their wilder impulses, to offend them from time to time, perhaps even to frighten them. But if so, it is not because they are not self-regulating to begin with; it is because, like an animal that has a mind of its own, they regulate themselves only too well—in a direction that is contrary to our own interests and that may in fact lead to our downfall.

Two Avatars of Torture

Consider the following exchange between a journalist and two members of the U.S. House of Representatives, one a Democrat and the other a Republican, recently heard on American television:

> JOURNALIST (speaking to the Democrat): How do you explain the Obama administration's desire to increase taxes for the richest Americans and not to lower them? The richest are the ones who create *jobs* and you want to throttle them?
>
> DEMOCRAT: What's stalling the economy is a lack of demand. People aren't buying!
>
> REPUBLICAN: If people aren't buying, it's because they *anticipate* losing their jobs, or that they are going to be unemployed for a long time.

What we have to do is create jobs, and therefore help the small and medium-size businesses that create them!

DEMOCRAT: But why should they create jobs if they *anticipate* that the demand will not be there to buy what they will produce?[36]

The sharpness of the disagreement, the clash of claims and counterclaims, gives the impression that two irreconcilable views are in conflict. Sophisticated listeners would have interpreted the Democrat's remarks as a Keynesian explanation of the crisis: firms anticipate insufficient demand, and so produce less—and therefore offer fewer jobs—than they could. This state of affairs can be remedied only by increasing demand, for example through higher wages. The Republican, for his part, makes the case for supply-side economics: he takes the side of firms, for which the cost of labor is always too high. To his way of thinking, unemployment is the result of overpriced labor and excessively burdensome taxation.

From the Republican point of view, the two participants in this debate cannot both be right. If there is unemployment, it is because the price of labor is too high by comparison with that of commodities. The relative price of commodities being too low, the problem is not one of excess capacity, but rather of insufficient production (in which case, of course, contrary to fact, one should see lines of people outside stores). What is more, such a disequilibrium could only be temporary: since the law of supply and demand operates on the labor market no less than the market for commodities, the relative price of labor should drop until both unemployment and excess demand for goods are eliminated.

From the Republican point of view, then, a general crisis of excess capacity is impossible.[37] This impossibility strongly resembles the one described by a joke that economists sometimes tell at their own expense. Two economics professors are out for a stroll when one of them sees a hundred-dollar bill lying on the sidewalk. "Impossible," says the other without even looking, "someone would have picked it up already." Just so, the type of crisis to which Keynes gave the name "deflation"—where workers cannot find jobs and producers cannot find buyers for their products—could not occur. Naively, one might suppose that both the Great Depression of the 1930s and the Great Recession of our own time proved the opposite. But if that were the case, there is an obvious and immediate solution that would be in everyone's

interest: as Henry Ford showed, firms have only to hire unemployed workers, pay overtime, and increase wages, and in this way distribute a purchasing
power that will naturally absorb the increase in production. Maurice Allais
memorably likened the effect of this policy to a fleet of helicopters raining
paper money down upon a dumbfounded populace.

Ah, money. This is where the shoe pinches—and where the Democrat
might have seen the advantage of granting his opponent's argument while
making it serve his own. Economic agents find it hard to communicate.
Indeed, in the standard theory, they communicate only by means of money.
Monetary exchange, as we have seen, makes it unnecessary for them to speak
to one another, and enables them to avoid cooperating, in the sense of comparing plans, sharing ideas, and working together. Money therefore suits the
individualistic, quasi-autistic purposes of the neoclassical economic agent
marvelously well—purposes that, as we shall see later, amount to a collective
lie. Money allows him to exchange information with other agents while at
the same time seeming not to do this. But the paradox of noncommunication
that nevertheless manages to communicate comes at a price. This brings us
back to Henry Ford. He hired unemployed workers, yes. But he did not pay
them in the form of an advance against the purchase of his own automobiles! He gave them money, which functions as money only through its very
abstraction, its character as a "universal equivalent" (to use Marx's phrase)
or general medium of exchange—a point on which Keynes (to whom I owe
the argument being developed here, and who otherwise seems to have been
wholly uninfluenced by Marx) was in full agreement. Money, as Keynes was
at pains to emphasize, is an advance against *any* commodity whatever. Henry
Ford therefore had no guarantee that the wages he paid would be converted
into a demand for his own cars. The orthodox economist may be more than
willing, of course, to grant that automobiles are not necessarily the first thing
unemployed workers will want to buy once they find work again; many of
them will want to buy meat and better housing, and this in turn will increase
the profits of butchers and real-estate developers, which will then be converted, at least in part, into a demand for automobiles. This argument can
only be pushed so far, however. In a modern economy, individual purchasing
power is distributed over so many interdependent sectors in such complicated ways that no manufacturer can be sure that the result of his increasing
production will not end up in a liquidator's warehouse somewhere.

Since agents in the neoclassical scheme of things do not speak to one another, they must find some other way to deal with the fundamental uncertainty of economic life. They do this by coordinating their behavior with reference to fixed points situated in the future. Keynesian deflation is one such point of reference, which the market brings forth through the mechanism of self-transcendence. A considerable power of attraction is exerted in this way, due to the mutually reinforcing behavior of two opposing poles, structural unemployment and insufficient aggregate demand. The Republican was right: households *do* anticipate a higher rate of unemployment, and cut back on their consumption as a result. But the Democrat was right as well: firms *do* anticipate a drop in demand, and cut back on hiring as a result. Firms and households therefore give each other more and more reason to believe that their course of action is justified by events.[38]

Economic life is filled with points of reference having the same bipolar structure. Consider the opposed and mutually reinforcing behavior of transportation and employment, one of the main sources of dysfunction in modern societies. The very same day the debate I have just described was broadcast on television in New York, as it happens, a local newspaper printed a brilliant cartoon. The cartoon has two panels. The two same figures appear in each panel, side by side. One of them speaks frankly about his true feelings, but with the look of a zombie, devoid of any visible emotion; the other listens to him with a dazed expression. In the first panel they are sitting together in a car, stuck in a traffic jam; in the second panel, they are sitting in an office cubicle. In the first panel the driver says: "I hate to drive, but I need a car to get to work." A few hours later—no longer surrounded by cars like his own, but by employees like him, prisoners like him—he says: "I hate my job, but I have to keep up the payments on my car." In the background, angry noise: horns furiously honking, in the first panel; in the second, a coworker barking from the next cubicle ("Shut up!").

Here, then, are two hells, familiar to millions of people from daily experience, which produce and strengthen each other in a vicious circle of counterproductive needs. The essence of capitalism resides in this fundamental fact: hell 1 and hell 2 are the same hell. Like evil itself, whose logic we examined in the first chapter, this minor hell functions by distancing itself from itself. It is self-justifying, since each of its two incarnations creates the other's necessity: work requires travel, and travel requires work. As it happens, "travel" has the same etymological root as the French word for work, *travail*. Both derive from the Latin *trepalium*, a three-pronged instrument of torture on which the unfortunate victim was impaled. Our words often know more than we do. The torture of work and the torture of travel are one and the same, only the torture assumes different forms.

The significance of this self-referential loop, and the reason why it arouses stunned looks and cries of rage, can be grasped only if one sees that it opens up a path to each of these two poles. The hard part is to understand *how* the loop opens up this path. For the automobile is not only the instrument of a necessity; it is also a promise of liberation. But the liberation is from an industrial hell that it has itself helped to create. Work is likewise not only the instrument of a necessity; it is a job, an occupation, a trade—in short, the promise of social recognition, of membership in a group. The question naturally arises, then, how much such a promise is worth.

Unnecessary or even harmful products are routinely justified by the number of jobs they are expected to create. The planned obsolescence of products and appliances, the squandering of nonrenewable natural resources, the wasteful consumption of energy, the reckless polluting of the environment—no one dares to oppose such things because they provide work for people who vote. In the 1970s, when I was working with Ivan Illich to dispel the great myths of industrial society,[39] a Communist labor union in France vehemently opposed attempts to cancel the Concorde program. No one supposed for a moment that the union sought to hasten the advent of a classless society in which former proletarians would travel by supersonic transport. It was fighting to protect jobs. At about the same time another labor union favored reducing social inequalities on the ground that it would increase consumption by workers and so, by stimulating growth, boost employment. Again, no one imagined that it was guilty of confusing the end with the means. The ultimate aim of industrial society is to create work, even though the economic rationality this work embodies makes it a form of torture—an evil that should be reduced as far as possible. This contradiction is the Gordian knot of capitalism. It can be severed only by changing the way we think about civilized life.

Political Self-Transcendence

If human beings were rational in the sense intended by economists, they simply could not form a political entity, for they would be incapable of placing confidence in one another or of managing their conflicts in a way that would not be destructive for everyone. Promises, threats, contracts, treaties—all these ways of creating what Hannah Arendt called "islands of predictability" and "goalposts of reliability" amid the fundamental uncertainty of human affairs[40]—would be beyond the power of men and women to contrive. If they do nonetheless succeed in living together in society, it is because they are able to throw off the yoke of economic rationality.

The justice of this view as a theoretical matter is unproblematic, as I will show in a moment. But its truth as a practical matter is increasingly perceived by economic agents themselves, many of whom now call for a renewed emphasis on ethical behavior so that the machinery of capitalism does not grind to a halt. But this demand, made even by some business executives, is misguided for at least two reasons. First, ethics is not treated with the respect it deserves when it is demoted to the status of a commercial lubricant. Second, asking ethics to solve a problem that is fundamentally political in nature entangles us in a category error. It may be objected that economic agents are immoral insofar as they behave selfishly, displaying neither altruism or generosity, concerned solely with maximizing their gains. But there is nothing in the least new about this. Capitalism, from its very beginnings, has seen selfishness as the energy source of economic activity.

The present crisis, in my view, is a truly novel situation. The old order was based on a singular discovery: agents who, at the outset, acted no more ethically than the *Homo economicus* of neoclassical theory nevertheless found ways of coordinating their behavior with reference to a common conception of the future; in so doing they created bonds of mutual trust that made it possible to prevent routine disagreements from spiraling into periods of protracted violence. The effect of the crisis has been to reveal the illness of which it is a symptom, namely, the incapacity of Economy to project itself forward in time. It is as though the future no longer provided any mooring, or fixed point, for planning; as though there were no longer any way of making the future present. Why should this be? Has the future become too uncertain?

No, people have always lived with the like of our present uncertainties. Is it because we have begun to doubt the very possibility of a common future? This is a more plausible suggestion, which I shall examine in the next chapter.

For the moment, however, I should like to consider the kind of reasoning that will be required to establish the truth of the view I have just stated. It is a kind of reasoning that is unfamiliar to economists, but well known to logicians and metaphysicians, even to theologians. The idea that the foundations of Economy can be properly examined using the methods of theology, rather than of economics itself, may seem odd, but surely it is more honest than smuggling theology in through the back door, as economists typically do. This aspect of economystification is in any case a complicated business, which I reserve for the fourth and final chapter. The topic of nuclear deterrence, which I take up briefly in the appendix, is knottier still.

The rational agents of neoclassical economic theory—technically speaking, individuals who seek to maximize their self-interest within a given possibility space—have no reason to trust one another. To show that they are nevertheless able to overcome this obstacle by coordinating their behavior with reference to the future—and in this way to reach a higher level of rationality—we need only consider a very simple situation that preoccupied Hume and Kant, and indeed a long line of philosophers from Hobbes up to the game theorists of our own day. It involves two agents who are prevented from making a mutually advantageous transaction because the two phases of the transaction cannot be executed simultaneously. The problem is that one agent must make the first move: he must hold out his hand in the hope that the other will respond in the same way. But what reason does he have to take the initiative in a world where, by hypothesis, no sense of obligation or duty—and therefore no sense of indebtedness—exists? There is nothing to stop the other agent from keeping what he freely offers without handing over anything in return. The first agent realizes this, and concludes that the best course of action from his point of view is to offer nothing. Even if the other agent were to promise to play his part in the transaction, there would be no reason to take him at his word: confidence is a futile gesture in the absence of elementary norms of responsibility and trustworthiness. The whole problem of indebtedness, which has become the chief obsession of capitalism in its present form, under the domination of finance—the paralyzing fear that debtors will not pay back what they owe, and therefore that the chronic anxiety caused by this uncertainty will never come to an *end*[41]—is contained in miniature in this little fable of the transaction that never takes place.

Let us suppose, however, that the two agents finally succeed in coordinating their behavior through a prophetic future, that is, a future that has been foretold in the technical (and wholly secular) sense I mentioned earlier. It may be that they owe this conception to an actual prophet, or perhaps merely to conversation with each other. However this may be, they are henceforth subject to the condition on which the loop connecting present and future depends: the projected future must be such that the purely self-interested reactions its anticipation elicits do not make the causal production of this future impossible. This condition is the mark of self-transcendence: it excludes the case in which one agent makes the first move and the other refrains from making the next one; for the first agent, having anticipated the other's defection, would not have given him the opportunity to defect by himself making the first move. From this mode of reasoning there results a kind of categorical imperative: Never act in such a way that, your action having been anticipated by another, your actual performance of the action would be *causally* impossible. Mutual exchange satisfies this condition. It is the rational solution to the basic problem encountered in trying to bring about a self-transcendent future. There is no need of any sort of ethical nudge to persuade individuals to cooperate.

This is hardly an academic point. Once upon a time there was a very French political institution that had more or less succeeded in devising a mode of democratic deliberation that would favor the emergence of a self-transcendent future: the economic planning carried out under the direction of the Commissariat Général du Plan for four decades after January 1946. As far removed from the Soviet Gosplan as it was from neoliberal laissez-faire ideology, planning in France until the mid-1980s aimed (in the phrase of one of its founders, the economist Pierre Massé) at "achieving by concerted deliberation and study an image of the future that is sufficiently optimistic to be desirable and sufficiently credible to give rise to actions that will bring about its own realization."[42] This formula expresses in its own way exactly the situation I have sought to describe in speaking of a secular prophet. The prophet is aware that the future causally depends on the way in which it is anticipated, including the way in which it is described and publicly presented. His words bring into existence a miraculous form of coordination based upon a shared conception of the future that is capable of closing the loop between the causal production of the future and its self-fulfilling expectation. The example of French-style planning nevertheless introduces a decisive novelty: reflexivity no longer comes into being through an intermediary, the exceptional individual who is revered as a prophet, but through the deliberation of the body politic as a whole.

This specific institutional embodiment of the idea of self-transcendence suggests that a self-transcendent future can be produced, at least in principle, by exploiting the dominance of politics over economics—a relation that itself depends on properties of self-transcendence that are peculiar to politics. The result of democratic deliberation goes beyond the intentions of any particular citizen, beyond any of the various arguments that may be deployed in the course of debate. Such deliberation is often imagined to take place in the mind of a collective subject, the people or the nation, in order to convey the idea that it cannot be reduced to any one particular will (as Rousseau would have said), for it transcends all particular wills. This is evidently an abusive way of speaking, for there is no subject endowed with consciousness and purpose who wishes what the people wish for, no particular will that coincides with the general will. What this way of speaking is trying, unsuccessfully, to put into words is nothing other than the model of self-transcendence.

To show that writers on politics have been concerned since the earliest times with the concept of self-transcendence, but nevertheless have seldom managed to give it anything resembling proper expression, would require a book of its own. It will be enough for our purposes here to note that the difficulty first became acute in the work of the founder of modern political philosophy, Thomas Hobbes. Hobbes's hypothetical reconstruction of the genesis of the state assumes that individuals in a state of nature wish for civil peace, but are incapable of obtaining these things by themselves. Each person has an absolute "right to all things." In the aggregate, however, these rights cancel each other out, creating a mood of impotent rage that culminates in a "Warre of every one against every one" (*bellum omnium contra omnes*). Hobbes's solution to this problem is the construction of an "Artificiall man," Leviathan, which is to say an absolute sovereign, a "Mortall God."[43] The sovereign's authority is constituted by a contract, or rather a multitude of bilateral contracts among individuals, by the terms of which each person relinquishes his unlimited right to all things at the same time as everyone else, in favor of a third party, who, although it is not a partner to all these contracts, guarantees that they will be respected. The sovereign's power is absolute. Indeed, it is the greatest power that can be imagined by mortal men.

Thus it is supposed that individuals in a state of nature, which is to say a state of mutual hostility, find the means to create a power that infinitely surpasses their own. In order to have the thing they most desire—peace, protection against violence—they are obliged to step outside themselves by means of a transcendent figure, an external source of authority that they have themselves created. This figure, Leviathan, is the only one allowed to reserve for himself what the others have renounced: the unlimited right to all things.

Hobbes's theory misunderstands how self-transcendence operates. That a similar misunderstanding should be found in a nearly opposite theory of social contract, due to Jean-Jacques Rousseau, is revelatory. Whereas Hobbes meant to justify absolutism—even providing a theoretical foundation for it, and therefore for a sort of absolute transcendence—Rousseau sought to do the same for the concept of direct government of the people by the people, dispensing with representation or mediation of any sort. This meant ruthlessly eliminating any trace of exteriority, any hidden mechanisms, any cleavage between the body politic and the people. The result is a world of absolute immanence. It is well known that the concept of the general will was supposed to resolve what Rousseau himself called the "great problem of Politics, which I compare to that of squaring the circle in Geometry."[44] Rousseau nevertheless ended up making law, as the expression of the general will, structurally analogous to Hobbes's Leviathan: legislation must have, in relation to men themselves, the same exteriority, the same overarching and comprehensive reach (as a consequence of "plac[ing] the law above man")[45] as the laws of nature—even though it is men who make their own laws, as they well know. As in Hobbes, this state of affairs is paradoxical in the pejorative sense of the word: it constitutes an enigma to which there is no obvious solution. What is more, Rousseau's political thought in its various historical incarnations, from the Terror to the totalitarianism of the twentieth century, produced monstrous forms of pseudotranscendence—the result of Rousseau's own inability to make the body politic both transcendent and immanent in relation to the people. Here we have another case of failed self-transcendence.

The thinker who came closest perhaps to the model of self-transcendence I have in mind, disposing of its paradoxes and relying on internal political mechanisms alone, is Alexis de Tocqueville, whose analysis of the despotism of public opinion in democratic societies (and especially the one he had studied at first hand, in the United States) remains an unequaled tour de force. Tocqueville begins by explaining how social equality—which he calls "equality of conditions"—led Americans spontaneously, and almost inadvertently, to adopt the same philosophical method, namely, of "search[ing] by oneself and in oneself alone for the reason of things."[46] He goes on to say this:

> As for the effect which one man's intelligence can have upon another's, it is of necessity much curtailed in a country where its citizens, having become almost like each another, scrutinize each other carefully and, perceiving in not a single person in their midst any signs of undeniable greatness or superiority, constantly return to their own rationality [and so] to the most obvious and immediate source of truth. So, it is not merely trust in any particular individual which is destroyed, but also the predilection to take the word of any man at all.
>
> Each man thus retreats into himself [and] from [there] claims to judge the world.[47]

And yet, ultimately, the need to appeal to some higher authority is inescapable. This authority cannot be rooted in any kind of transcendence, for democracy, insofar as it consists in equality of conditions, implies the rejection of all exteriority: "It is only, therefore, with great difficulty that men who live in times of equality are led to place outside and above human bounds the intellectual authority to which they submit. Normally they seek the source of truth in themselves or in their fellow men."[48]

We therefore seem to find ourselves at an impasse, for authority can come neither from the outside nor from other human beings. Tocqueville's solution to the problem of squaring the circle is this: authority is derived from a third party—a party that is not any one person in particular and that appears to each member of society as something outside him, though without being outside society as a whole. This third party is evidently the result of a process of self-transcendence: a point of reference that everyone helps to create, but that each person sees as standing above and apart from him.[49]

It is, in other words, the production by the system itself of something that transcends it—in the present case, public opinion. Tocqueville's account of how it emerges, and of the despotic regime it imposes, constitutes a very fine introduction to the idea of self-transcendence itself:

> Gradually, as citizens become more equal and similar, the inclination for each man to have a blind belief in one particular man or class lessens. The predisposition to believe in mass opinion increases and becomes progressively the opinion which commands the world.
>
> Not only is commonly held opinion the only guide to the reason of the individual in democracies but this opinion has, in these nations, an infinitely greater power than in any other. In times of equality, men have no confidence in each other because of their similarities but this very similarity gives them an almost limitless trust in the judgment of the public as a whole. For it appears likely, in their view, that, since they all have similar ideas, truth will reside with the greatest number.[50]

All this, Tocqueville concludes, points to the "immense pressure of corporate thinking upon the intelligence of each single man."[51] But does the "judgment of the public as a whole," what Tocqueville calls the *esprit de tous*, refer to a collective subject? Certainly not. Tocqueville remained firmly committed to the principle of methodological individualism, long before anyone had heard of the phrase. As in the case of many other collective phenomena that behave like quasi-subjects, public opinion emerges from a process of self-transcendence. A general theory of such phenomena would also explain the emergence of the state, whose excessive concentration in France furnished Tocqueville with the occasion for another masterly piece of analysis, as well as a variety of things that greatly inconvenience orthodox economic theory, not only money, trust, and conventions,[52] but also the elusive notion of business confidence, to which Keynes assigned a preponderant role in his explanation of the Great Depression.[53]

Both political theory and economics come dangerously close here to behaving like the neighboring disciplines they tend to look down upon, such as sociology and psychology, particularly with regard to the analysis of crowd behavior. As I insisted earlier in connection with the problem of communication in an age of catastrophe, the resemblance among these various disciplines arises from the fact that they all rely, wittingly or not, on the logic of self-transcendence, which requires that the impact of a prophecy on public opinion be integrated into the prophecy itself. But this causal link is subject to the laws governing human collective phenomena, not to the laws of economics or (in the case of climate change) the thermodynamics of the upper atmosphere. I would even go so far as to suggest that it is because the idea of self-transcendence has never been properly worked out, and its properties never systematically investigated, by theorists whose minds it has nonetheless always haunted that it has become customary to distinguish two basic methodological tendencies: individualism and holism. The model of self-transcendence does not, strictly speaking, come under the head of either one, since it joins the individual level with the collective level, and vice versa.

Let us recall what one of the earliest exponents of methodological holism, Émile Durkheim, had to say in this connection. In *The Elementary Forms of Religious Life* (1912), considering the position of the orator, an eminently political figure, Durkheim undertakes to analyze

> the special attitude of the man who speaks to a crowd—if he has managed to enter into communion with it. His language has a kind of grandiloquence that would be absurd in ordinary circumstances; his gestures are overbearing; his thought itself is impatient with order and easily becomes carried away in all sorts of extreme pronouncements. He feels filled to overflowing with an overabundance of forces that spill out around him. Sometimes he even feels dominated by a moral power that is larger than he is, for which he is merely the interpreter. This quality marks what is often called the demon of oratorical inspiration. This unusual surplus of forces is quite real: it comes to him from the very group he is addressing. The feelings provoked by his speech return to him inflated and amplified, reinforcing his own. The passionate energies he arouses echo back to him and increase his vitality. He is no longer a simple individual speaking, he is a group incarnate and personified.[54]

Even a superficial reading of this splendid piece of phenomenological description cannot fail to notice the power of the bond that is established between the speaker—classically, a political leader—and his audience. Yet a more attentive and analytical reading stumbles over what appears to be a contradiction: does the speaker dominate the audience or is he dominated by it? Durkheim's own words can be cited in support of both views. The model of self-transcendence that peeks out from behind his analysis resolves the tension, making it clear that the crowd puts itself above and beyond itself through the figure of the leader.[55]

It would be absurd to suppose that, because political thought has found it no less difficult than economic thought to elaborate a model of self-transcendence, politics is not an essential source of self-transcendence. The more interesting, and far more difficult, question is why politics should have this power. The answer is not in doubt, as far as I am concerned. As I have argued elsewhere, it is owing to what remains of the sacred in politics that it possesses the power of inspiring a people, now and then, to raise itself above itself and to project itself into the future.[56]

In the economic sphere, everything has its price—even politics. More and more openly today, as we saw earlier, Economy buys politicians, without for a moment making a secret of the pride it takes in doing this. Sometimes it boasts of being able to do without politicians altogether; other times it is content to delegate minor tasks to them. Economy takes great pleasure in inspiring fear in them, and in being feared by them in turn. Nothing delights it more than to see these puny creatures creeping about, terrified of making the slightest misstep or doing anything that might anger it in any way. But Economy makes a grave mistake. In degrading and neutering politics, it deprives itself of the means by which it might lift itself out of the swamp of managerialism into which it has now sunk, without even noticing it. Condemned to the pointless immanence of corporate housekeeping, and having no other horizon than the immediate future, it retreats into itself, unconcerned to give the young any reason to live, unmoved by the spectacle of whole populations reduced to hunger and misery. No longer able to contain violence, it confidently takes the world by the hand and leads it into the future—a still more horrifying future than the last.

CHAPTER 3

The Economics of the End and the End of Economics

All days travel toward death, the last one reaches it.

—Montaigne, *Essays* 1.20

For better or for worse, Economy is propelled into the future by the force of self-transcendence. When Economy succeeds in going beyond the pitiable condition of mere managerialism, letting itself be carried away by the transcendent power offered to it by politics, it is for the better. But when it drags politics down to its own level, and converts leaders into servants, Economy loses the exteriority it must have in order to flourish and signs its own death warrant.

Capitalism can avoid extinction only by persuading economic agents that an indefinitely long future stretches before them. If the future were to be closed off, a reverse domino effect would abolish all economic activity from the moment its end point became known. With the approach of the end, trust would be impossible since there would no longer be any time to come in which debts could be repaid, and money would lose all value since no one would accept it in payment of outstanding obligations. This argument may be extended backward from the ultimate to the penultimate moment, and then to the one before that, and so on all the way back to the present moment. But what would happen if it were believed that the world will soon come to an end—without either the day or the hour being known?

The Time That Is Left to Us

Belief in the Apocalypse appears to be more widespread just now, in the early part of the twenty-first century, than ever before. The only difference—an enormous difference, it must be conceded—from earlier, almost forgotten ages is that in our age it is not, or not only, members of gnostic sects who warn that the end of time is drawing near, but also scientists, engineers of various kinds, even a far-sighted statesman or two. So many clouds have gathered on the horizon by this point, it is difficult to say that their pessimism is unfounded. The way forward has now been hidden from view, if it is not actually blocked.

Human beings have traditionally destroyed themselves in one of two ways, either through civil strife, war, or other forms of conflict (the very idea of which, as Clausewitz observed, entails an escalation of violence to the point of mutual annihilation),[1] or by making the physical conditions of survival unsustainable. The difference between these two types of threats is now being eroded, along with other distinctions that humanity has long taken for granted as points of moral reference. Once there was a clear separation between natural catastrophes, catastrophes caused by the evil that man deliberately visits upon his fellow man, and catastrophes caused by technological or industrial accident. The weather, for example, still occurs in the writings of economists as a metaphor for randomness, something that is immune to human intentions, desires, and plans. Today, however, we know that human activity affects the weather as a result of climate change. If we destroy nature, is it because we hate nature? Of course not—we merely hate one another. The furious dynamic unleashed by what economists are accustomed to call growth, assuming it is always and everywhere something to be desired, is responsible for what might with equal euphemism be called the collateral damage of progress now that nature has become one of the victims. But the first serious manifestations of global warming will not be random fluctuations in weather patterns (including local episodes of cooling), nor rising sea levels, the thawing of glaciers in the Andes and the Alps, the disappearance of the permafrost layer in Siberia, the melting of the Arctic ice floes, the expanding reach of drought to some of the world's most productive agricultural regions, the increasing frequency of so-called extreme events (typhoons, cyclones, tornadoes, flooding), and so on; instead, the first manifestations will be large-scale population movements provoked by the anticipation of these disasters. Population movements will in turn beget conflicts and wars, as violence and the destruction of nature become caught up in a self-reinforcing loop.

The accidental emblem of this growing inability to make what used to be familiar distinctions is the catastrophe at Fukushima that plunged Japan into mourning on the fateful day of 11 March 2011. In calling it a "second nuclear disaster," the writer Haruki Murakami, one of Japan's most prominent intellectuals,[2] unmistakably linked this event to Hiroshima. What is more, the catastrophe itself unleashed a chain reaction of calls for an end to reliance on nuclear power. In the absence of massive and coordinated investment in renewable energies, however, rising worldwide demand for energy in the decades to come ensures that any move away from nuclear power could only further aggravate the threat already posed by climate change. Earlier I recalled Günther Anders's amazement more than fifty years ago on discovering, during his visit to Hiroshima and Nagasaki, that the survivors of the catastrophe apparently felt no resentment toward the human beings who had caused it. They regarded the disaster as a natural catastrophe—as a tsunami.[3] What an irony of fate! At Fukushima it was an actual tidal wave, the most tangible and unmetaphorical wave imaginable, that awakened the nuclear tiger. In this case, of course, the tiger was caged. An electronuclear reactor is not an atomic bomb; indeed, it is in a sense the opposite of one, since it is meant to control a chain reaction that it itself has triggered. In the realm of the imagination, however, a negation affirms what it denies. In reality, the other realm that we inhabit, the tiger escapes from its cage from time to time. Fukushima was all at once a natural, industrial, and technological catastrophe—and, owing to the associations it conjures up in the mind of an entire people, a moral catastrophe. Fukushima was the herald of a new age.

In recalling Hiroshima, Fukushima reminds us that the gravest threat weighing upon the future of humanity remains the military threat: the atomic bomb. The conditions that once made deterrence effective, or at least apparently so, are no longer satisfied in an age of nuclear proliferation and terrorism, with the result that the taboo against using the bomb grows weaker with each passing year. Advances in miniaturization and ballistic technology trivialize atomic weapons, so that they now seem to be a weapon like any other. Under these circumstances it is hard to imagine that the explosion of such a device in a city somewhere would not have the effect, sooner or later, of letting the genie out of the bottle. No one can say what then would happen.

All this leaves the vast majority of economists completely unmoved, of course. A few of them spend their time analyzing what they are pleased to call "risks," refining the conceptual tools described in textbooks in the chapter devoted to rational choice under uncertainty and occasionally permitting themselves a brief skirmish over some aspect of the precautionary principle. But there are not many even of those. It is still possible today to describe oneself as an analyst of economic growth without causing other economists to double over in laughter, much less anyone outside the profession who is incapable of making the least sense of elaborate mathematical models that amount to nothing more than intellectual camouflage, a way of giving an air of authority to exercises that are as pointless as they are abstruse. Each time a crisis seems to have been brought under control, the members of the economic establishment hasten to congratulate themselves that the worst did not come to pass—scarcely suspecting that the very rails on which capitalism rides once more, owing to their selfless and tireless efforts, will soon carry it back to the edge of the cliff. Their smugness is intolerable, their self-satisfaction ridiculous, and their optimism obscene.

But why do businessmen, industrialists, bankers, financiers, investors, and all the others who make the global economy work seem to show no interest in taking apocalyptic prophecies seriously? Presumably for a reason that is exactly the opposite of Pascal's wager: betting on apocalypse carries with it the risk of missing out on investment opportunities—possibly fabulous opportunities—if the apocalypse does not in fact occur; if it does occur, everything goes down the drain, and the world with it. Either way, one stands to lose. On closer examination, however, the premise turns out to be false: capitalists do in fact take the apocalyptic perspective seriously, even if they are not really aware of it. Curiously, it is because they do take it seriously that they exhibit a form of optimism that the former chairman of the U.S. Federal Reserve, Alan Greenspan, famously denounced in warning against the "irrational exuberance" of markets. What explains this apparent paradox?

The puzzle arises from the peculiar temporal structure of a certain kind of expectation, the feeling we experience in awaiting the occurrence of a catastrophe that is bound to occur, only we do not know when, neither the hour nor the day. The outstanding example of such a catastrophe is our own death. How much time we have left to live is wholly unknown. Why else are we so haunted by the problem of time, if not because we know that our death is inevitable? It is not death in general that is our chief worry, but our own death—the death that is ours alone, death in the first person: *my death!*

Experiencing *my* death would not be possible were it not for the fact that every human life is punctuated by a series of what might be called little deaths—interruptions, breaks marking the end of a period, a cycle, or a phase of existence that often seem catastrophic to us, in the original sense of the word, the conclusion of a story: vacations that come to an end, a love affair that is broken off, a job that is lost. One's own death is the supreme example of a catastrophe foretold, but there are many others. The time we are confronted with here is the time that elapses while we wait for a catastrophe to occur that is inevitable, but whose precise date cannot be named, whether the catastrophe is my own death or the death of capitalism.

Economy and Death

Nothing more plainly reveals economists' astonishing insensitivity to the most basic aspects of the human condition than the way they treat matters of life and death. Since economic theory is defined for the most part by its method, rather than by its subject matter, economists suppose there is no subject to which this method cannot profitably be applied. The death of a person is just another topic for analysis, no less suitable than inflation or unemployment. It may nevertheless well be the fatal stumbling block of Economy, the snare and delusion that brings it face-to-face with its own final collapse.

The branch of applied economics in which death figures as an object of analysis is better known as health care economics. Let us begin by considering the remarkable fact that a very substantial share of individual medical expense in developed countries is incurred during the last year of life.[4] As a recent study put it, with an air of detachment bordering on apathy, a person's "proximity to death has a considerable impact on the level of health care expenditure."[5] Note that it is not the patient's age that interests us here. Since the probability of dying normally increases with age, there is no need in principle to assume that expenditure increases *directly* with age, all other things being equal, in order to detect a positive correlation between age and spending on health care. As an empirical matter, however, both age and the approach of death do appear to contribute to the level of expenditure.

However this may be, economists and physicians who cite the study's finding seldom do so without qualification. While acknowledging that end-of-life care undoubtedly has some palliative effect, they argue that its chief value is symbolic, and that its effects on mortality and morbidity are negligible. Enormous amounts of scarce resources would therefore be saved by preparing patients to meet their certain end by traditional methods that allow them to live out their days in the company of family and friends, and by restricting costly medical procedures to demonstrably effective interventions. More than one medical expert has bluntly asked whether it makes sense for a country to manage its health care budget in a way that encourages older people to refuse to accept the reality of dying at the expense of programs aimed at improving access to health care and education among the young.

My early research on medicine and health policy, strongly influenced by the thinking of Ivan Illich, with whom I collaborated throughout the 1970s, was concerned with many of the same questions. We began by asking why it was that France then led the world in consuming prescription drugs. The most alarming figure, at least from the point of view of the government health-insurance system, which commissioned our study, was the annual rate of growth in such consumption (more than 17%), more than half of which was due to the rate of growth in the average price of prescription drugs (roughly 10%). The rise in drug prices was itself the result of unnecessarily frequent updatings of a compendium of officially approved pharmaceutical preparations. On average, new drugs cost much more than the ones they replaced; indeed, almost half of the gross revenue of the pharmaceutical industry came from products introduced within the past five years. What disturbed public health officials most, however, was that fewer than 5% of these allegedly new medicines could truthfully be said to augment the existing stock of approved drugs. The majority of them were combinations of known substances or derivatives of previously patented molecules, when they were not actually identical to a product already brought to market by another manufacturer under a different name.

The question therefore arose whether wastefulness of this sort was solely the result of a lust for profits on the part of pharmaceutical companies, or whether consumers were not partly to blame as well. This raised a further question. Who is the consumer in this case? The one who takes a drug, without paying for it; or the one who prescribes the drug, without paying for it either? It seemed to me at the time that the willingness to recommend a new medicine is a *sign* that the doctor communicates to the patient, but also, and especially, to himself—a sign that he has heard the plea for help that the patient has addressed to him, even if the plea has not been put it into words.[6] The philosopher Jean-Claude Beaune later expressed the same idea this way: "The doctor will never really answer the question—the only question—that the patient puts to him, which amounts to this: 'Tell me that I'm not going to die.' He cannot answer it, but he cannot help but hear it."[7] It is by means of a technological sign—a new medicine—that the doctor attempts to deal with a question that is not in the least technological.

The rationality of end-of-life medical care is not without its defenders within the economics profession. Gary Becker, at the University of Chicago, became famous for extending economic analysis to domains that appear to be the furthest removed from the world of the market. Deciding whom to marry and how many children to have, how often one goes to church, whether to park one's car in a no-parking zone or to kill one's mother-in-law with arsenic—all these things can be analyzed in economic terms, which is to say weighed in terms of costs and benefits. Whoever weighs something assumes the existence of a common measure or standard of weight. But what unit of measurement are we to choose when it is a matter of comparing a fine levied in a certain currency with the time needed to carry out a given task or the leisure time of prisoners, or comparing eternal life in heaven and in hell, or comparing sex for money and romantic love? The answer, of course, is the dollar. All human values—not only ones having directly to do with health, but also those associated with the pursuit of happiness, the desire to receive an education, the freedom to live as one pleases, and so on—are reducible to a single question: how much are you willing to pay for this value? The explanations contrived by Becker and his many epigones are baroque, sometimes grotesque. But this has not prevented the profession from awarding him its highest honor, the Nobel Prize, in 1992, and the U.S. government from awarding him the National Medal of Science eight years later.

What price is a bedridden old woman on death's doorstep willing to pay to have her life prolonged by a few months? Her entire life savings, quite obviously, since they will do her no good at the bottom of her grave. The price her family and friends are prepared to pay is even greater, Becker says, for one must not forget the immense sorrow they will feel on having a loved one taken away from them before her time. Comparing the monetary value of staving off death a bit longer with the cost of keeping the patient alive, one arrives at the comforting conclusion that "under these circumstances, a high level of expenditure for terminal care may be considered consistent with collective preferences and therefore *efficient according to the criterion of economic rationality*."[8]

I leave it to the reader to reflect further upon this deeply humane sentiment and turn now to a more difficult problem. When one talks about the medical expenses that are "incurred during the last year of life," this predicate can scarcely have any economic implication, for in the majority of cases the end point of this last year is—and can only be—known in retrospect, that is, after the patient's death. *Hora incerta, mors certa . . .*

Statistical Death and Counterfactual Death

An evil genie paid a visit to the president of a certain country and made him the following proposal: "I know that your economy is sluggish. I desire to help you strengthen it. I can place at your disposal a fabulous technological invention that will double your gross domestic product and increase the number of jobs by the same amount. But there is a price you will have to pay. Each year I will demand the lives of 20,000 of your people, a high proportion of them young men and women." The president recoiled in horror and dismissed his visitor at once. He had just rejected the invention of—the automobile.

This allegorical fable is familiar to many law students in the United States. What does it show? That if modern societies so readily accept the evil of highway fatalities, if it does not seem to them to pose any particular problem of conscience, it is precisely because they never think of it in these terms. The fable allows us to perceive the presence of a classic moral dilemma, involving the sacrifice of innocent victims on the altar of the collective good. Traditional moral philosophy, although it is obsessed by this type of problem, has never succeeded in satisfactorily dealing with it. And yet one has only to naturalize the elements of the dilemma in order to make it completely disappear. Once the flows of automobile traffic are subsumed under the laws of hydrodynamics, the resulting statistical regularities take on the appearance of fate. It is only on this condition that health care policy in the broad sense (including everything that comes under the head of public safety) can be formulated; that budgetary choices can be rationally justified; that the "value of human life" can be discussed in economic terms without provoking public outrage.

Let us suppose that we have available to us a budget of ten million dollars that is to be allocated between two activities, the aim of which in each case is to save human lives—say, medical research on cancer and the improvement of roads and highways. Let us also suppose that the return on investment in each case is decreasing: the more money that is invested in either cancer research or road repair, the higher the cost of saving an additional human life.[9] Let us suppose, finally, that the point of the exercise is to maximize the number of lives saved. Given this much, it is a simple matter to demonstrate mathematically that when this maximum point is reached, the cost of the additional human life that one has given up trying to save as a result of placing a cap on the total budget is the same in the two domains. If this were not so—if the cost were higher, for example, in the domain of health than in the domain of safety—then transferring resources from the first domain to the second would increase the total number of lives saved. It is exactly this cost that economists call the value of human life. The recognition of such a value entails at least two things: first, that life has a price—a *finite* price—since in each domain one is obliged to abandon the attempt to save human lives for the simple reason that resources are finite; second, that the finite value thus assigned to human life satisfies an optimality requirement with regard to the allocation of resources among the various domains in which action is contemplated.[10]

In all of what I have just said, one thing must be kept in mind. The human lives that are added and subtracted as though they were so many tomatoes or leeks are mostly, though not always, *statistical* lives in the sense they have in the fable that I quoted at the outset. As an empirical matter, what does one observe? In the first place, unsurprisingly enough, that efforts to save additional lives in each domain where action is possible are curtailed beyond a certain point: in the one case, heroic measures are restricted and end-of-life care is limited for the most part to the relief of pain and suffering; in the other, effective but very costly antiterrorist security systems go unfunded. After a certain point the search for possible survivors in the rubble of a town leveled by an earthquake is called off. Meanwhile, aid programs to the third world are unable to pay for relatively inexpensive ways of fighting malaria.

The second thing one observes from experience is that the criterion of optimal resource allocation, on which the concept of the value of human life ultimately rests, is massively violated. The discrepancies between the implicit values of human life in the various domains in which governments and private agencies can intervene are simply gigantic, in some cases approaching ratios on the order of 1:10,000. Can reality really be this irrational? It is more likely, I believe, that the concepts we use to understand it are hopelessly inadequate.

When I was a student at the École Polytechnique in Paris I wrote a paper about the optimal management of the fleet of jeeps maintained by the French army. This was the heyday of what was called operational research, an American invention during the Second World War that involved the application of rather elementary mathematics to problems of management and organization. I do not believe that I was wrong in concluding, rather obviously as it may seem, that beyond a certain period of service it becomes necessary to retire old jeeps and replace them with new ones. My practical recommendations were more sophisticated, since they were illustrated by a curve showing that the optimal maintenance schedule varies with a vehicle's age: the closer one comes to a programmed end, the less point there is going to the trouble of repairing major breakdowns and the more sense it makes to anticipate having to replace the vehicle.

Again, I leave it to reader to imagine the horrified reaction that economic logic of this sort would elicit if it were to be applied to a fleet of human beings.

It would counsel us to give up caring for patients after a certain age, and to leave the dying to their fate. I am well aware that Nietzsche, in *The Twilight of the Idols*, proposed a "morality for physicians" that advocated exactly this policy: "A sick person is a parasite on society. Once one has reached a certain state it is indecent to live any longer. Vegetating on in cowardly dependence on physicians and their methods, once the meaning of life, the *right* to life, has been lost, should be greeted with society's profound contempt. The physicians, for their part, ought to convey this contempt—not prescriptions, but every day a new dose of *disgust* at their patient."[11] When Nietzsche wrote these words, however, he was himself on the verge of madness.

The considerations that lead economists, in the name of rationality, to allocate resources in such a way that the value of human life is the same in every domain of public policy are the very ones that prevent us from telling jeeps and human beings apart. The statistical life that one saves is no more human than a motorized vehicle. It has no personality, no name, no age, no sex. This is what makes it substitutable for any other statistical life. Indeed, it is doubly *absent* from the world of actual human beings: in the first place, precisely because it is a statistic—no one has ever seen an "average man";[12] but also because the statistical life that is saved has only a virtual—or, as we should rather say, using the technical term, a counterfactual—existence. What would have happened if one had refrained from acting to prevent illness or fatal accidents? People would have died, real persons with singular personalities. But if one does act, no one can say *who* would have died if one had not acted.

Depending on the population sample in question, and particularly on its size, one statistical life may be interpreted as having more or less weight than another. It is this fact that explains, at least in part, the considerable differences one observes in the implicit value of human life assumed by policymakers in giving or withholding their approval of various lifesaving measures. What is more, the counterfactual character of a statistical life means that the dissolution of personal identity in calculations aimed at maximizing the number of lives saved may be more or less complete, depending on the circumstances. The thirty-three miners trapped for more than two months during the summer of 2010 at the bottom of a mine in the Atacama desert in Chile may perhaps have taken some consolation in seeing that a considerably higher value was now placed on their lives than had implicitly been attributed to them beforehand, when they were still no more than numbers in an undifferentiated population of miners. But for people throughout the world who sympathized with their agony, and probably also for the Chilean government, which had staked its reputation on getting them out alive, their individual identities were merged with that of the group to which they belonged. One may well imagine that if 90% of them had been rescued, the world would have joined the government in considering that, under the circumstances, it had fully discharged its duty. The families of the three miners who would have perished no doubt would have felt differently.

The statistical dissolution of personal identity assumes another form in the case of preventive (or, as it is now more common to say, precautionary) action. This is explained not only by the counterfactual character of the lives saved, but also by the indeterminacy of the future. And yet here again we find ourselves faced with a question of more or less, and it is this gradation that explains, if it does not justify, the enormous discrepancies that one observes between the implicit values of human life from one policy domain to another. Consider the problem of deciding how best to spend a given amount of money for the purpose of preventing transportation-related fatalities. Although highway accidents each year account for a considerably greater number of deaths than airplane crashes, the circumstances of *each* highway accident, as compared to the circumstances of *each* airplane crash, lead us to assign a much greater moral weight (if I may be permitted such an expression) to the statistical life one has given up hope of saving in the case of airplane crashes than in the less spectacular case of highway accidents. On the highway one dies alone in one's car, or perhaps with a few passengers. The victim of a crash of an Airbus 380, on the other hand, has some eight hundred companions in misfortune. It is not surprising that the implicit value of a human life should be considerably higher in the second case than in the first.

It is plain, then, that the enormous observed differences in the cost that society refuses to bear in order to save an additional life are a result of discrepancies in the value attached to human life that arise from the dissolution of personal identity, to one degree or another, in the realm of the statistical and the virtual. But not to health care economists, who continue to defend the usual methods of cost-benefit analysis on grounds of rationality—as though they were incapable of distinguishing between a human being and an army jeep. In the professional literature one sometimes encounters a distinction between death in the third person ("his" or "her" death) and death in the second person ("your" death). The fact that the physician, in relation to his patient, finds himself faced with this second-person situation may seem to suggest that human life, from the medical point of view, has no price; that is, its value has no upper bound. But everything we have just considered shows that this way of looking at the matter neglects a whole range of intermediate situations that need to be taken into account.[13] It will perhaps not come as a surprise that not even death in the first person—"my" death, the most intimate relationship to death we can have—has escaped the tender mercies of statistical analysis.

Expecting Catastrophe

When I was a child, I thought that death was a continuous passage from one state into another, a gradual crossing over into unconsciousness: the senses grow dull, the body loses its strength, the faculties slowly dim. There is no radical break in this transition, no discontinuity, no catastrophe—no more than when water, the moment it reaches a critical point, passes without any discontinuity from the liquid to the gas phase. Today I believe that nothing could be more false. One dies at the very moment when one wishes most to live. Jean de la Fontaine expressed the same idea marvelously well in his fable "Death and the Dying Man." The moral of the fable is just this: "Most loath to die are those most close to death."[14]

Death is a catastrophe foretold. Atropos, the inexorable fate of Greek mythology, the one who cuts the thread of destiny, merely neglected to tell us the hour and the day. Our ignorance has incalculable consequences. Some people welcome it, believing that it permits them to live more freely, for they liken an unknown end to an indeterminate end, and so to the absence of an end. "Whatever certainty there is in death," La Bruyère remarked, "is mitigated to some extent by that which is uncertain, by an indefiniteness in time that has something of the infinite about it."[15] Others are troubled by the thought that this indeterminacy may keep them from knowing themselves. One thinks of the story told of Jorge Luis Borges, on being asked yet again by an interviewer to say something about himself. "Say something about myself? But I know nothing about myself—not even the date of my death!" Knowing what we know now, we may imagine having been there when the interview took place and, availing ourselves of the future perfect—that miraculous tense that transforms the future into the past—saying to ourselves, "When Borges dies, seven years and three months will have elapsed since he made this memorable remark." But this is a luxury that was not available to Borges himself.

It is this waiting period, the time that stands between us and a catastrophe whose occurrence we know to be inevitable but whose exact date is unknown to us, that I wish now to examine more closely. Paradoxically, although the catastrophe will come as a surprise the moment it occurs, the fact that it will come as a surprise is not, or should not be, a surprise. We are aware of heading inexorably toward the end, but since its precise location is not known, we can always hope that the end is not yet near. Then, suddenly, without warning, it sneaks up on us when we least expect it. The most interesting case involves a traveler who finds that the farther he advances along his route, the greater the *objective* reasons he has for supposing that the time that remains before he reaches his destination *is increasing*—as if the end point of his journey were moving away from him more rapidly than he is approaching it. In this case, in other words, it is when, without knowing it, one is nearest to the end that one is justified in believing that it has never been farther away. The surprise is total. And yet since one already knows all of this, it ought to be nil. Time therefore pulls in two opposed directions: on the one hand, we know that the longer we travel the nearer we draw to the end; on the other, since the moment when the end will be reached is unknown to us, we find it difficult to regard this end as being fixed. In the cases to which I now turn, the longer one goes on without seeing the end, the sounder are the reasons one has for thinking that fate, or perhaps a lucky star, has pushed back the final moment.

The first example concerns a person's life expectancy at a given age, which is to say the average number of years that someone of that age has left to live. It is tempting to say that the time left diminishes as one grows older, but this is not necessarily true. The life expectancy of a child of a certain age, which is to say the average number of years he has yet to live,[16] may *increase* with age. The fact that he has managed to survive the critical stage of the first years of life is a *sign* that his constitution is robust and therefore that he will live a long life. Here again, the knowledge that in growing older one inexorably draws nearer to the end tugs on the thread of life from one side, and the inference that the end is receding faster than one is approaching it tugs on the thread from the other.

Infant mortality is a quite particular case. In developed countries it long ago ceased to be a serious public health problem (though it is true, alas, that the richest among them, the United States, scarcely does any better in this category today than a third-world country such as Brazil). Consider the more general case of an adult in the prime of life who suddenly learns that he is suffering from a grave illness, cancer, say, or neurovascular disease. He may find some reassurance in consulting mortality tables, not for the population as a whole, but for the subset of those who have suffered from the same illness in the past. The further the date of the original diagnosis recedes into the past, the smaller the probability of a recurrence and the greater the average number of years of life that remain—until, of course, a turning point is reached.

There is something puzzling, then, about the kind of temporality we are considering here. A mathematical concept, "fractal" shape, will help us make better sense of it. A figure is said to be fractal if it is self-similar on every scale of observation. The late Benoît Mandelbrot, certainly one of the most powerful and original minds of our time, to whom this concept is due, showed that it applies to a whole class of shapes found in the natural world, the best known of which may be snowflakes and the coastline of Britain. Not incidentally, perhaps, the concept first occurred to Mandelbrot in the course of analyzing probability (or frequency) distributions.

The most familiar such distribution is what most people call a "bell curve."[17] If I toss a coin two thousand times in a row, the number of heads will, on average, be a thousand. Probably it will not be exactly a thousand, but it will very likely be located within a relatively narrow range lying on either side of this number. Extreme events—only a few hundred tails, or more than fifteen hundred tails, out of two thousand coin tosses—cannot be excluded, of course, but the bell-shaped curve assigns an exceedingly low probability to them.

Individual trials (in this case successive coin tosses) are observed to converge upon a normal distribution when they are causally independent of one another. The probability of the next toss being tails will always be equal to one-half, even if the preceding tosses have overwhelmingly been tails. All this is well known, at least tacitly, even by those who are bored to tears by statistics. In modern democracies, where no issue can be decided without a sampling of public opinion having been made first, statistics are unavoidable. But now things become both more complicated and much more interesting.

For several years now, another type of distribution has occupied the attention of specialists. It is found everywhere catastrophic natural events threaten to occur: raging rivers in Europe and North America, hurricanes in the Caribbean basin and the Gulf of Mexico, volcanic eruptions and tsunamis in the Indian Ocean, forest fires in California and along the Mediterranean. It is also found in the world of finance, with the expansion and bursting of speculative bubbles. Although this type of distribution attaches a relatively low probability to extreme events, the chance is nonetheless considerably higher than the one assigned by the bell curve. The statistical weight of a random event, as we have seen, is the product of its magnitude and its probability. If events of very great magnitude are assumed to have a small—but by no means infinitely small—probability, the prospect of a major catastrophe, though it remains comparatively unlikely to occur, cannot help but weigh heavily in our assessment of future risk. Inevitably, the shadow cast by its very possibility darkens our outlook.

A simple thought experiment will make it clear why this distribution (which I have so far refrained from identifying by one of its several names) should be, if not universal, then at least characteristic of the events that are of most pressing concern to us today. Imagine that ten thousand coins rain down from the sky, falling uniformly over an area in which a hundred buckets have been placed to catch them. If coins are assumed to land independently of one another, the distribution of coins per bucket will conform to the bell curve. The number of coins landing in most of the buckets will be close to the average, which is to say a hundred; only a few buckets will contain several dozen coins or, by contrast, several hundred of them. Let us now change the conditions of the experiment, and assume that the larger the number of coins found in any given bucket, the greater the chance that more coins will fall into it. Under this assumption, the distribution of coins over the set of buckets as a whole now takes on an entirely different appearance: the deviations from the mean allowed by the bell curve become amplified by a self-reinforcing dynamic, with the result that the probability of extreme events occurring is considerably increased.[18]

This distribution takes one of its names from the sociologist Vilfredo Pareto, who together with Léon Walras formed what came to be known as the Lausanne School, the cradle of neoclassical economics. Pareto was interested in comparing national patterns of personal income distribution. In every country, and on every scale of wealth, he observed that the ratio of the expected value of individual incomes above a given level to that level is constant. Let us assume the ratio is 1.3. This means that the expected value of incomes higher than the minimum wage, for example, is equal to 1.3 times this wage; and also that the expected value of incomes greater than the salary of a trader at a Wall Street investment bank, for example, is equal to 1.3 times this salary. If, as the Stiglitz-Sen Commission's report on the indicators of happiness rather unsubtly suggested,[19] money brings happiness only as a consequence of its relative value, this means that happiness is equally distributed over all social classes. Our thought experiment more vividly illustrates the same principle of distribution: the more coins a bucket already has, the more new ones it will attract. Similarly, in the case of a Pareto distribution, the wealthier you are, the greater your chance of becoming wealthier still.

A Pareto distribution is fractal, which is to say self-similar on every scale of observation—in this case, for any value above which the distribution is observed. This is why the average of the values higher than a given value exhibits a constant relationship to this value. The case I considered earlier, of the distribution of life expectancies in a country where many children die at birth or in the first months of life, illustrates this property.

Mandelbrot sought to convey some sense of the special character of fractal distributions by means of a very fine parable.[20] Imagine a land that is permanently covered by disorienting mists and fog, and which contains a great many bodies of water. Some are no more than ponds; others resemble lakes, still others seas. An expedition of surveyors and cartographers is sent out from a neighboring land of lakes whose distribution with respect to size is fractal. Coming upon what appears to them to be a lake, they set out to cross it in a boat. Owing to the fog it is impossible to see the far shore. They assume from their experience of their own country that the size of the body of water they are rowing across likewise obeys a fractal distribution.

The longer the explorers row across the lake without reaching the opposite shore, the larger they are justified in believing the remaining distance to be—as if the horizon were receding faster than they were approaching it. They reason in the following way: the already considerable amount of time that has gone by without the opposite shore coming into view suggests that we are crossing one of those extremely large expanses of water to which the fractal law assigns a sizable weight; therefore it is likely that there is still a much longer way to go than we had thought at first. The idea of an eternally receding horizon is an illusion, of course, since the explorers cannot doubt that the lake has a definite size and that the distance separating them from their destination is a fixed quantity. They know that sooner or later the opposite shore will come into view. Yet when they pause to compute the expected value of the distance still to be covered, they are bound to conclude that they are further away than the last time they estimated this distance.

The explorers' confusion reaches its height just as they are on the verge of seeing the opposite shore, for it is then that they believe they have never been further away. What is more, the longer they have been rowing, the more startled they will be when this moment actually arrives. The fog in Mandelbrot's parable of the receding shore is the equivalent of what Günther Anders called "the blindness before the Apocalypse."[21]

Surely this, or something very much like it, must have been Bernard Madoff's state of mind as he sailed the high seas of financial banditry. The broader the base of his pyramid scheme became, with the increasingly successful recruitment of new clients, the greater his confidence that the rewards would continue to grow—so long, of course, as he was not caught. And yet he could not be unaware that one day the end would come, and that his scheme would collapse like a house of cards. The longer the scheme worked, the more terrible the surprise was bound to be.

It is not by chance that I take the example of financial speculation. No one doubts for a moment that Madoff was dishonest. But it would be both unfair and misleading to place special emphasis on a single swindler. Mandelbrot, quite early in his career, had studied what might be called honest financial speculation, and showed both as a theoretical and an empirical matter that speculative phenomena generally are governed by a fractal law. In the euphoric "boom" phase, as the bubble begins to expand, the more optimistic investors are, the greater their reason for looking forward with still more optimism. Indeed, it is just when the bubble is about to burst that the euphoria reaches its highest point.[22]

The theory of extreme events that I have just sketched is hardly new, and it has been confirmed by experience many times over. What is more, it is known to many influential figures in the financial world. Anyone who is not acquainted with it should be ashamed of his ignorance.[23] If we assume that informed economic agents are a majority, the question arises whether awareness of the theory would change their behavior. This is a vexed question, fraught with doubt and difficulties. Prudence therefore dictates a maxim: the greater one's reasons for optimism, the more one owes it to oneself to fear catastrophe and to guard against it, for the end is undoubtedly near. As a theoretical matter, this double bind is resolved by recognizing that, while optimism is rational at one level, doomsaying is rational at another, which transcends the first, for it looks out upon the future from the point of view of the end of the voyage that lies ahead, and not of the voyage as it unfolds. I call this form of prudence "enlightened doomsaying."[24] It involves an act of imagination by which one looks ahead, to a moment *after* the extreme event has occurred, and contemplates the path leading to it from a perspective that combines surprise at the event's occurrence with foreknowledge of this same surprise—which is to say, the recognition that the event is certain to occur.

For a philosopher, the idea of telling someone he is going to be surprised calls to mind a famous paradox.[25] Here is one of its forms. On a Sunday a man is sentenced to death and told that he will be hanged one morning in the coming week, without the day being named. This warning is accompanied by a prediction, which will turn out to be a diabolical trap: on the day chosen for the execution, when the executioner comes at dawn to bring him to the scaffold, the condemned man will be surprised. He is then taken back to his cell, where he racks his brain in the poisonous hope of discovering when his existence will come to an end. It seems obvious to him that it cannot be the following Sunday. For in that case he would still be alive at noon on Saturday, and therefore in a position to deduce that his hanging will take place the following morning—in which case he would not be surprised. He therefore crosses Sunday off the list of possible occasions. But now it is Saturday's turn to be dismissed. Since Sunday is no longer a candidate, the very same logic will hold good at noon on Friday, assuming the condemned man is still alive then. On applying this reasoning to each of the remaining days of the week, he becomes convinced that none of them can be *the* day, and therefore that he will not be executed. And so when the executioner comes to get him at dawn on Thursday, he is completely taken by surprise—just as he had been told he would be.

Whatever may be the logical virtues or defects of this argument, it plainly depends on the existence of a known end or term: the life of the condemned man will not last longer than the next Sunday. But it is precisely this condition that does not obtain in the capitalist world. Torn between hope and despair, Madoff expected nevertheless that the stream of new clients would continue to grow. Speculators, for their part, counted on the subprime bubble to go on expanding forever, and the desperate Americans who mortgaged their entire future in order to buy a house looked to the unlimited increase in its value in order to be able to pay for it. What makes capitalism possible is the belief that it is immortal. What may be called the original sin of capitalism lies concealed in the fact that the future must endlessly stretch out before it if, at any given moment, it is to be able to deliver on its promises. This is the source of the cult of growth. For the capitalist system to function satisfactorily at any given moment—which is to say, for full employment to be achieved—agents must anticipate that its expansion will go on indefinitely.[26] The lesson of Mandelbrot's parable is that the longer the final reckoning is postponed, the more surprising its inevitable occurrence will be.

The world's leaders have, as I say, succeeded in putting the capitalist locomotive back on track. For the moment its progress is halting; but as it picks up speed, the more hopeful they will become and the more firmly they will believe in a radiant future. It is at precisely this moment that they ought most to distrust their reasons for optimism. For catastrophe may be lying in wait for them just around the bend.

Economy at the Apocalypse

We have just seen that optimists owe it to themselves to be catastrophists, precisely because they are optimists. Conversely, there is good reason to believe that the wild optimism displayed by economic agents during the most recent financial crisis, and not least of all by government officials, was fed by a catastrophism that dares not speak its name.

The argument I am about to present is due to one of the most insightful commentators on the crisis, the financier Peter Thiel.[27] A cofounder of PayPal, the world's largest e-payments company, Thiel went on to become a principal investor in Facebook while still a young man. His perspective is that of an enlightened doomsayer. Unlike armchair philosophers such as myself, however, he has put to the test of experience investment decisions that are based on explicit assumptions and rigorous analysis (and not, it should be added, on mathematical models so complex and so opaque that they have acquired something like an autonomous power of decision).

Thiel was impressed in the first place by the wholly novel character of speculative bubbles over the last twenty years or so, considering both the circumstances under which they have formed and the violence with which they have burst, one after another. The euphoric phase, no less than the crash itself, displays the characteristic features of extreme events—so strikingly, in fact, that even the laws of fractal distribution seem incapable of explaining them. Just before the Japanese real estate bubble burst in the late 1980s, the Tokyo Stock Exchange accounted for half the world's market capitalization. The Land of the Rising Sun seemed destined to rule the earth, or so many believed. The brief reign of Japan, Inc. was followed by the still vaster Internet bubble of the late 1990s—the most enormous boom the world had ever seen. No one could have imagined that it would be succeeded in its turn, five years later, by a global real estate bubble of even greater magnitude.

Some analysts see such events as the result of the irrational exuberance of markets; many more blame the greed of traders and their love of profit—as if this were something new. On all sides, intellectual laziness and incuriosity take refuge in moral indignation. We will be better served, I believe, by trying instead to uncover the deeper causes of our current predicament.

In the kingdom of money, as Thiel is well qualified to observe, the apocalyptic perspective has few champions; indeed, there is still less sympathy for it there than in society as a whole. What appeal could the idea that capitalism is mortal possibly hold for an investor? If capitalism were to die, nothing would any longer have value. If its end were to be predicted, and the date of its demise announced, the prophecy would be immediately falsified, for in that case, the possibility of an indefinitely long existence having been denied, catastrophe would strike at the time of the prediction and not at the predicted time. The alternative, a far more attractive one, is to act as though capitalism is immortal. And yet as Thiel shows, while at the same time introducing a new paradox, this does not mean that the apocalyptic perspective has not exerted an immense influence on the calculations and behavior of investors. Quite the contrary.

The survival of capitalism is today indissociably linked to the success of globalization. But what would the failure of globalization signify? That the forces of antiglobalization had triumphed after all? Thiel dismisses this suggestion, for in his view antiglobalization is part and parcel of globalization, and cannot exist apart from it. Paraphrasing Tocqueville, one might say that globalization draws its strength from everything that opposes it. Globalization bears the marks of a providential dispensation: it is universal, it is enduring, it escapes human power at every turn; events, no less than human beings, all serve to promote its development. If globalization fails, this can only be the result of a major catastrophe, whose collateral damage will include the end of capitalism. This catastrophe would resemble more or less closely the one whose broad outlines have been sketched by doomsayers such as myself.[28] The human destruction of nature and the ceaseless escalation of organized violence conspire to cast the very survival of humanity in doubt. The most terrifying threat of all, widespread nuclear conflict, continues to be the greatest threat of all.

Thiel does not believe that economic and financial agents permit themselves to contemplate the prospect of catastrophe directly. They eliminate it from their calculations, on the ground that it is too horrible to bear close scrutiny. But it is precisely in removing it that they give it a place; in fact, a quite considerable place. In trying to make sense of this second paradox, it will be instructive to make a simple calculation. Imagine an investor who is keenly aware of the threat to humanity, but who nonetheless does not wish to factor it into his assessment of future outcomes. Intuitively he understands that the path capitalism must travel in order to survive is like the crest line in an alpine landscape, beyond which lies the abyss. Let us suppose that the probability this investor tacitly assigns to the optimistic scenario—the survival of commerce under successful globalization—is 10%. If he anticipates that a certain business will one day be worth $100 per share, as long as the optimistic scenario comes to pass, what price should he be willing to pay for it today? Presumably 10% of $100: multiplying probability by magnitude, he arrives at a valuation of $10. Note that this calculation completely neglects the other branch of the alternative, which implies disaster for all investors. If a 90% probability of global catastrophe were taken into account, not only would the expected value of the share be negative; the anticipated loss would be infinitely negative! This deliberate neglect lies at the heart of Thiel's paradox. During the most recent great bubbles, investors have not valued such shares at $10, but at much higher amounts, no doubt in many cases close to $100. Indeed, disregarding the catastrophic scenario altogether has the consequence that in any possible world in which investors survive, the share price will turn out to be $100. In that case its anticipated value should logically be $100 as well.

This sort of reasoning calls to mind a humorous advertisement for the French national lottery some years ago that cited a statistical study showing that 100% of past winners had bought a ticket. Thiel insists, however, that one must not lose sight of the psychological context surrounding the formation of recent bubbles. If investors risked so much of their money on the success of Internet firms in the late 1990s, it is because the alternatives seemed to them frighteningly bleak. If America's new class of paupers, all those who were to see their savings vanish with the collapse of share values, rushed to take advantage of subprime mortgages, it is because they saw this as the only way to avoid certain destitution in old age. Could it be that these people, in conducting their own optimistic thought experiment, showed more foresight than their neighbors? That in projecting themselves into the only conceivable future that was not catastrophic, and thereby granting it the probability of a sure thing, they did what had to be done in order for it to have a chance of coming about?

We are now in a position, then, to appreciate the full implication of Thiel's paradox. Ultimately, it was the apocalyptic perspective that drove investors to desperately embrace an attitude of unrestrained optimism. I very much fear that the analysis I have proposed here confirms the wisdom of enlightened doomsaying: the desperate embrace of unrestrained optimism grows out of a diffuse, unreflective catastrophism; and this, in turn, justifies us in adopting a rational form of catastrophism.

CHAPTER 4

Critique of Economic Reason

A man actualizes himself only in becoming something definite, i.e. something specifically particularized; this means restricting himself exclusively to one of the particular spheres of need. In this class-system, the ethical frame of mind therefore is rectitude and *esprit de corps*, i.e. the disposition to make oneself a member of one of the moments of civil society by one's own act, through one's energy, industry, and skill, to maintain oneself in this position, and to fend for oneself only through this process of mediating oneself with the universal, while in this this way gaining recognition both in one's eyes and in the eyes of others.

—G. W. F. Hegel, *Philosophy of Right*

Economy is in danger of losing forever the very qualities that might make it a moral and political economy. In its contest of strength with politics, each victory economics achieves is a Pyrrhic victory. In its determination to conquer positions of power in the name of expertise, each one more elevated than the last, it sacrifices to a collective tutelary deity, the markets. But how many former heads of Goldman Sachs will have to be installed as chiefs of state in order to slake this nervous and insecure god's unquenchable thirst for reassurance? It is, as I have said, a losing battle. By reducing political life to the status of a mere servant, Economy little by little loses its capacity for self-transcendence, and in this way slowly but surely prepares its own demise.

We saw earlier that economic reason can be reconciled with political reason if individual agents are able to coordinate their behavior with reference to a common conception of the future. The conditions under which this can be done are primarily logical and metaphysical in nature, but there is an anthropological element as well. If it were to prove that these conditions were no longer satisfied, or, worse still, that they can no longer be satisfied, we would have good reason to believe that the power of Economy to provide a political solution to the problem of violence, the problem from which we started out, has finally been exhausted. In that case our predicament would be grave indeed, since we would then have to brace ourselves for the advent of a posteconomic phase of modernity. I trust that the rather technical character of the argument I am going to develop in the pages that follow will not obscure this fundamental fact.

Coordination by means of the future entails that agents all take the same future as being fixed. Recall that I use the term "fixed" in relation to an action or event in the sense that the future is counterfactually independent of this action or event. No matter what an agent does, he assumes that his action will have no counterfactual effect on the future even though it is causally responsible, in part, for bringing it about. If he were to have acted differently than in fact he did, in other words, the future *would have been* the same. This future is a fixed point, a common point of reference for everyone.

Coordination by means of the future therefore combines freedom of individual choice with something that can only be called predestination. It is what allows economic reason to have its intended effect, what allows us to hope that Economy may yet be made reasonable once again. One cannot help but think in this connection of Max Weber's famous—and famously controversial—thesis in *The Protestant Ethic and the Spirit of Capitalism* (1904–05). In the course of revisiting Weber's argument we will be led, as though in a game of dominos, to overturn a number of well-established metaphysical and rationalist principles, one after the other, and so finally to consider the question of faith—not omitting its negative variety, aptly named "bad faith" by Jean-Paul Sartre.

It is a truism, or at least it should be one, that no economy can function without confidence in the future. And yet this deceptively vague and enigmatic expression conceals a great wealth of insight. In subjecting it to careful scrutiny, we shall see that two fundamental assumptions are knocked down in rapid succession: first, the causalist hypothesis, with the result that free agents are shown to be capable of exercising a certain type of power over the past even though, of course, they have no *causal* power over it; and second, a basic axiom of the economic theory of rational choice, the strategic dominance principle.

The Irrationality of the Calvinist's Choice and the Dynamic of Capitalism

Weber's thesis, that there is a vital link between what he called the Protestant ethic and the spirit of capitalism, has never been more disputed than it is today. Sociologists and historians do not tire of attacking it, whether on grounds of logical consistency or empirical adequacy. It is the question of consistency that primarily interests me here. Weber's thesis has the form of a paradox. But a paradox is neither an inconsistency nor a contradiction; it has a distinctive and stable identity of its own. And yet it may assume various guises. Weber's paradox has the same form as what I have called the mark of the sacred. The discredit from which Weber's thesis suffers today is less the result of the empirical evidence its critics have marshaled against it, which they wrongly imagine to constitute a devastating refutation, than the consequence of a profound misunderstanding of its logical structure.[1]

Weber did not maintain that Protestant countries are the chosen land of capitalism and of economic development. For anyone of his time, as for us today, that much went without saying—or would have done, were it not for the misleading claim of Latin countries to a share of the credit. The historian Pierre Chaunu invites us to compare maps from 1560 and 1980:

They can almost be superimposed. What was done was never undone. Everything happened between 1520 and 1550. Once drawn, the boundaries between the Reformation and the Counter-Reformation never really moved. The maps from the middle of the sixteenth century and the end of the twentieth century are 95% superimposable. Let us rank the countries and regions in descending order of per capita income and of investment in research and development. Let us then, following the now classic [*sic*] classification of W. W. Rostow, rank these countries and regions in order of their date of entry into the stages of take-off and sustained growth. At the top of the list, more than 80% of the time in either case, we find countries with a majority Protestant population or a predominantly Protestant culture and, in the leading places, a Calvinist tradition.[2]

Weber's argument is much more precise and circumspect. It seeks to demonstrate, first, that there exists a causal relationship, or perhaps merely an elective affinity (it is rather difficult to say exactly what Weber had in mind), between the Calvinist dogma of predestination and the *spirit* of capitalism; and, second, that this spirit is a necessary, though by no means sufficient, condition for the development of capitalism. It is not the explicit ethical teaching of Protestantism that fashioned the capitalist spirit, according to Weber, but the unintended and unexpected influence exerted by its implicit doctrinal assumptions on anxious minds.

Let us begin by examining the logical structure of Weber's argument and then go on to consider his analysis, not of Calvin's doctrine itself, but of the way in which the Puritans of New England reinterpreted it as a function of their social and cultural environment, on the one hand, and of their individual and collective psychology, on the other. On the Puritan view, a divine decision, irrevocable for all eternity, has assigned each of us to one of two camps, the elect or the damned, without our knowing which. As human beings we are powerless to alter this decree; there is nothing we can do to earn salvation, much less to deserve it. Divine grace is nevertheless manifested by signs. They cannot be observed by means of introspection, however; access to them can be had only through action. The most important of these signs—as Lutheranism was the first to insist—is the success achieved by putting one's faith to the test through labor in a worldly "vocation."[3] This is a trial and an ordeal both, for it requires the faithful to work tirelessly, continuously, and methodically, without pausing to rest once wealth has been amassed, without ever enjoying its fruits. "An unwillingness to work," Weber says, "is a sign that one is not among the saved."[4]

The "logical" response to this practical problem, Weber remarks, could only be "fatalism."⁵ The fatalistic choice of an idle life, marked by an unwill-ingness to work, is in fact the rational solution, since *whatever the state of the world may be*—in this case, whether one belongs among the elect or the damned—there is nothing to be gained from submitting to the grueling and costly business of doing righteous deeds. A rational choice theorist would say that one is dealing here with a "dominant strategy," in the technical sense that this strategy turns out to be the best in *every possible scenario*. And yet Weber's whole book is an attempt to explain why and how "the broad stratum of ordinary [Puritan] believers"⁶ made the opposite choice. Calvinist pastoral guidance advised that it was "a matter of duty pure and simple for believers to *consider* themselves among the elect few and to repel every doubt about their state of grace as nothing more than the temptations of the devil." This type of advice seemed plausible, Weber says, "because a lack of self-confidence was believed to result from insufficient faith; and insufficient faith results only from the insufficient effects of God's grace."⁷ Self-confidence, the means of assuring one's state of grace, could be attained only through "work, and work alone."⁸

The quarrel between Lutherans and Calvinists is still of the highest inter-est today. The Lutheran charge that Calvinists had reverted to the dogma of "salvation by good works [*Werkheiligkeit*]"⁹ provoked outrage, for it identi-fied Calvinist doctrine with the very thing Calvinists abominated above all else: Catholic doctrine. This amounted to saying that anyone who is prepared to acquire the *signs* of grace through unremitting toil and trouble reasons *as if* these signs were the cause of salvation—an attitude closer to magic than to reason, the Lutherans insisted, since it mistakes the sign for the thing it represents, namely, divine election. Hence the historical and anthropological paradox that a doctrine that in its origins was wholly antimeritocratic should have produced a highly meritocratic society, dedicated to the proposition that one must deserve to be saved.

The Calvinist's choice therefore appears to be irrational, and this is for two reasons that may in fact be one and the same: on the one hand, his choice violates what would appear to be a minimal criterion of rationality, the stra-tegic dominance principle; on the other, it seems to issue from a magical style of thinking. But it is here that Weber's argument seems plainly to contradict itself. For it attempts to show that ascetic Puritanism constitutes the logical conclusion of a vast historical process of disenchantment (*Entzauberung*) that repudiated "all *magical* means [for attaining] salvation as superstition and sacrilege."[10] It is this Puritan conception of existence, Weber maintains, that "stood at the cradle of modern 'economic man,'" gave birth to "*economic rationalism*," and transformed the "calculating spirit" of capitalism "from an instrument used in economic transactions into a *principle* for the entire *organization of life.*"[11]

But economic rationalism in this sense stands in flagrant contradiction to one of the least controversial axioms of rational choice theory, indeed an axiom that is entirely in keeping with common sense. Must we therefore conclude that the disenchantment of the world is itself nothing more than a magic trick? The confusion of Weber's critics on this point is perfectly understandable, and one is almost ready to forgive them for busying themselves instead with more respectable theories. Nevertheless I believe that they are wrong, and that by clearing up what at first sight appears to be a logical contradiction it will be possible to isolate a deep truth of anthropology.

Note, first of all, that Weber himself opposes logic not to anthropology, but to psychology. His remark about fatalism, to which I referred a moment ago, occurs as part of a larger observation: "Viewed *logically*, fatalism would naturally follow, as a deduction, from the idea of predestination. However, as a consequence of the insertion of the idea of 'conduct as testifying to one's belief [*Bewährung*],' the *psychological effect* was exactly the opposite.... [T]he chosen are simply, on the basis of their [e]lection, inoculated against fatalism. Indeed, they testify to their chosen status precisely in the act of turning away from the fatalistic consequences of the idea of predestination; *quos ipsa electio sollicitos reddit et diligentes officiorum* [their election itself causes them to be attentive and diligent in performing their duties]."[12] If one interprets fatalism in a way that is consistent with the strategic dominance principle, as I have done, the sign that one has been chosen is that one enjoys the *freedom* to violate this minimal principle of rationality. In that case, the *deliberate* choice of irrationality would appear to be a very unpromising foundation for the emergence of what Weber calls "economic rationalism."

One must nonetheless be careful not to misconstrue what Weber actually says. Most of Weber's critics identify fatalism with the renunciation or negation of free will: since God has chosen for us, we are no longer able to choose. Here the critics confuse a point of theological debate with the question that interested Weber, namely, how believers in a particular time and place went about trying to solve a very *practical* problem. It is true that Christian theology has often taken the view that the doctrine of grace, itself closely related to the idea of predestination, justifies the inference that free will does not exist. This conclusion, that free will and theological determinism are irreconcilable, is what philosophers and theologians call "incompatibilist." But Weber's Puritans cared very little for fine scholarly distinctions: their first and foremost worry was to save their souls! What I wish to show is that the choice that Weber calls fatalistic and that, moreover, he regards as self-evidently constituting the logical solution to the problem posed by predestination, is in fact a *compatibilist* response, no less than the apparently illogical response that Weber ascribes to the very great majority of Puritans. In each case, choice rests on the idea that predestination and free will are not logically contradictory.

Here we encounter the first and most serious error of interpretation committed by Weber's critics, which leads on to a whole series of confusions and false puzzles. Take, for example, the question of whether Puritan teaching is consistent with Weber's thesis or whether, to the contrary, it demonstrates its futility. The critics note among at least some authors and preachers what appears to be a curious indecision on a crucial point. One observes an oscillation between seemingly opposed positions: on the one hand, when these spokesmen of the faith expounded the dogma of predestination and its implications for the "certainty of salvation" [*certitudo salutis*]—a question to which they attached the very greatest importance[13]—it was not to works that they mainly referred, but to the subjective experience of faith; on the other, when they turned to matters of religious practice, they set predestination aside and appealed to the free will of the faithful, as if individuals were capable both of deserving and achieving salvation themselves. "We are therefore dealing with two types of discourse, each one largely autonomous in relation to the other," Annette Disselkamp concludes, "and not with the undivided view suggested by Weber."[14]

The case of the Presbyterian theologian Richard Baxter (1615–91) is particularly interesting. Baxter, whom Weber quotes at length, was accused by his fellow Puritans of flirting with Catholicism and, in particular, of substituting for the Calvinist dogma of justification by grace the "papist" dogma of justification by works. Works do indeed have an important place in his teaching: Baxter did not hold that the successes obtained through works are merely *signs* of salvation; he maintained that they make it possible to *acquire* salvation—a position that bordered on heresy. It can be explained by Baxter's opposition to one of the extreme forms assumed by the doctrine of predestination, known as antinomianism, which taught that trying to attain salvation, by whatever means, is a sin, for Christians are exempted from the obligations of moral law (hence the name of the doctrine) through grace and faith alone. "To Baxter's mind," one recent commentator has written, "an *improper* reliance upon the merit of deeds is far preferable to a *confident* trust in a justification which does not need to be demonstrated, a sincerity which does not need to be verified by self-scrutiny, a sanctification which need not be sustained by Christian *diligence*."[15]

Baxter's was not an isolated case. As the historian William Haller observed, Puritan preachers considered it their chief task to tell the faithful what they must do *in order to be saved*.[16] If one must deserve one's salvation, however, the implied existence of free will would appear to have replaced the dogma of predestination—which would amount to confusing Calvinism with another one of its heretical offshoots, Arminianism, associated with the humanist teaching of the liberal Dutch theologian Jakob Hermanszoon (better known by the Latinized form of his name, Jacobus Arminius). Arminius's emphasis on free will led him to advocate tolerance and, by contrast with those who defended the "fatalistic" doctrine of predestination, to favor commerce. It is a splendid historical irony that Arminianism should have been defeated as a political force by the orthodox Calvinism that traveled on the ships sent out from the United Provinces to trade with nations throughout the world.[17]

If we turn away from theological disputation and consider instead, as Weber himself did, the very practical problem of personal salvation, it will become clear that false dichotomies are all that remain. Just as fatalism, in Weber's sense, which is to say choosing the "logical" solution to the problem, is a choice made in complete liberty, albeit in the context of predestination, so the Puritan choice of *working* toward one's salvation is a predestined but nonetheless free choice. The blind spot of Weber's critics is that they can see neither freedom in the first case nor predestination in the second. This weakness is still more evident if we look at an earlier figure, the Puritan divine William Perkins (1558–1602). Perkins had developed a rational Protestant casuistry founded on the obligation to cultivate a "good" and "clear" conscience, untroubled by internal contradiction and serenely confident of God's presence. Works, it would appear, play no role in any of this. As Disselkamp puts it, "Election and the experience of election coincide."[18] Perkins, on the other hand, is interested in what he calls "means" of predestination:

> Whosoever are predestinated to the end [eternal salvation], they are also predestinated to the means, without which they cannot attain to the end: therefore as the elect necessarily at length do come unto the end, by reason of the certainty of their election: so also by reason of the same certainty, it is necessary that they should be traced through those means which tend to the same end. . . . And this is one of the chiefest uses of good works, that by them, *not as by causes, but as by effects* of predestination and faith, both we, and also our neighbours are certified of our election, and of our salvation too.[19]

The least one can say is that this passage gives more support to Weber's thesis than to his critics' claim that Puritanism measured the certainty of grace in terms of the subjective experience of faith. They can hold this view only by maintaining that here Perkins justifies works "*in spite of* predestination"[20]—even though he plainly says just the opposite. Already a century before Baxter, then, the adversary to be combatted was antinomianism and the peril of moral ruin that comes with it. As Perkins himself asks, in condemning this very doctrine: "If we be predestinate to eternal life, and our predestination be certain and unchangeable, what need we endeavour ourselves, believe, or do good works?"[21] Disselkamp believes she has found an error in his reasoning:

> The difficulty with which Perkins finds himself confronted is therefore not how to respond to the uncertainties of believers, but how *simultaneously* to maintain the dogma of predestination and the necessity of performing good works. He resolves the problem by affirming that, in the doctrine of predestination, the end (salvation) and the means (works) are inseparable, and that to be predestined to [enjoy] eternal life means that one is predestined to [employ] the means of attaining it. *There is, of course, a manifest contradiction here.* For if one is predestined to salvation, logically there are no "means" for attaining it. Nevertheless Perkins does not wish

to abandon these means, fearing that to do so would lead to moral laxity. He extricates himself from this difficulty by holding that means are not a matter of choice, but rather, no less than salvation itself, of predestination, and that they are not causes of it, but effects.[22]

Weber is therefore shown to have been wrong, but only because the exquisite subtlety of his argument has gone unappreciated—and its implication thoroughly misinterpreted!

Before examining the argument more closely, let us take stock of what we have so far established. It is clear that there is a risk from the point of view of moral law that an agent who is *free*, though predestined, makes the rational, antinomianist choice—the logical (or fatalistic) choice in Weber's sense, which is to say that he chooses the dominant strategy. Freedom of choice nevertheless does not prevent the predestined agent from making the other choice, from trying to attain salvation through worldly striving. This is what Perkins has in mind when he says that whoever is predestined to eternal life is predestined to have the means of attaining it; that he may resort to works in order not only to assure himself that he is saved, but also to bring about this salvation. Weber says nothing different when he holds that the chosen are protected against fatalism by virtue of their having been chosen; that in *rejecting* fatalism they both demonstrate and convince themselves of their election. There is no contradiction here, only the statement of a very logical argument, however odd it may appear at first sight. The means are predestined, and yet they are also the object of free choice. They are effects, not causes, and yet it is in choosing the means of predestination that the believer "chooses" predestination itself—not, quite obviously, because he produces it *causally*, but because he acts on it *counterfactually*, in the sense I gave this term earlier in connection with the idea of self-transcendence. Puritans who chose as the Calvinists did, who deliberately refused the "logical" solution, thereby endowed themselves with a counterfactual power over the past, notwithstanding that this same past continued to determine their present situation in the world. It is this choice that gave birth to what Weber calls economic rationality, but what from now on, in order to forestall any confusion with the technical meaning this concept has in rational choice theory, I shall call economic reason.

It is not my purpose here to argue on behalf of Max Weber's thesis in all of its aspects, only to defend it against grave misunderstandings. Weber himself could not entirely have succeeded in unraveling paradoxes that he seems almost to have devised simply for the sake of devising them.[23] Let us consider once again the opposition on which he insists between a "logical" solution (fatalism—the dominant strategy) and a "psychological" solution (worldly activity) to the practical problem posed by predestination. According to Weber, the Puritan's choice grows out of two things, the distress felt by the believer in the face of the most daunting questions of all—Am I one of the elect? If I am, how can I be sure?—and a correspondingly intense desire to be numbered among the chosen, to be spared eternal damnation. Weber's critics delight in emphasizing the implausibility, indeed the self-contradiction of such an explanation. Searching the historical record for empirical evidence in its favor, they find little or none. Did the Puritan faithful believe they had a kind of power over their election, according to Weber, or did they not? It is tempting to reply that they did, since they acted as though this were the case, by working to earn salvation. But in that case, their understanding of dogmatic teaching was corrupt, and it is not clear why they should have felt any distress. On the other hand, if the faithful did not believe they had such power, what sense are we to make of their behavior? As Disselkamp puts the point: "An individual deeply influenced by the dogma of predestination— and this, according to Weber, was true of a great many believers—would certainly not, being aware of the seriousness of what was at stake, seek to distort it. If he did, it could only be because he did not understand what it involved; but in that case, the intensity of the reactions Weber describes can hardly be explained."[24]

What, then, are Weber's critics really trying to say? They do not deny that many Puritans were racked by religious despair. While acknowledging that they were distraught, to the point sometimes of neglecting their duties, the critics maintain that they did not look upon works as a remedy for their troubles. And while the critics acknowledge, too, that the certainty of salvation was one of the most disputed questions among theologians, it was not in works, they hold, but in faith, that theologians sought the means of attaining it. Works did have some importance, of course, but only when preachers, faced with the hard facts of everyday life, sought to help those among their congregants whose conscience was wholly undisturbed by the thought of being unable to alter their fate see where their duty lay. Nowhere, then, does one find Puritans who were led by a wavering faith—the sign, according to dogma, of a problematic election—to take refuge in works; everywhere one finds fatalists (in the ordinary, non-Weberian sense of the term, that is, those who *surrender* to fate), some of them unhappy, the others either happy or indifferent. The commandment to perform works, to answer a calling in this world, was intended solely to awaken these happy or indifferent believers to the obligation imposed on them by moral law, which is to say the moral duty of rejecting fatalism.

This account nevertheless overlooks a plausible assumption, which, as it happens, is the blind spot of both Weber and his critics. The Puritan's resolve to choose the means of predestination was not at all a psychological choice. It was a *logical* choice—no less logical, and no less in accord with common sense, than choosing idleness. For Weber, the rejection of fatalism is a historical fact that can be explained in terms of psychological causes. For Weber's critics, by contrast, the rejection of fatalism is so little a fact, something so rarely encountered in Puritan communities, that preachers had to remind believers that it was their moral duty to reject it. But what if the behavior that Weber seeks to explain were not the rejection of the only "logical" solution to the problem of predestination, but instead *another, no less logical* solution to the same problem? In other words, what if the rejection of the dominant strategy (in this case, idleness) in favor of another strategy (industriousness) were not only compatible with the tenets of dogma, but actually constituted the "natural" response to the problem? In that case there would be no justification for converting one class of believers—what Weber calls "the broad stratum of ordinary believers"—into the heretics reviled by Calvinist doctrine.

Showing that this is in fact the case, as I shall now try to do, will at the same time resolve what earlier I called Weber's paradox. For if the Calvinist's choice is indeed consistent with economic *reason* and the spirit of capitalism in Weber's sense, and if it can be shown furthermore that this choice obeys another logic, a kind of rationality that is different from—and superior to— the rationality described by rational choice theory, then we will have succeeded in driving a wedge between this theoretical rationality and economic reason. What economists smugly imagine to be rational does not begin to rise to the level of what Weber calls the spirit of capitalism. Why? Because the rationality of rational choice theory produces a kind of behavior that is contrary to reason. If ever there was a time when capitalism was animated by a spirit, by a vital spark that could be likened to the winds of history (as Marx did, approvingly), it was only by elevating itself above this narrow-minded conception of rationality. Now, it may well be that the Puritans of New England did not behave in the main as Weber claims they did, and that their role in the rise of capitalism was much less important than he says. Let us concede as much for the sake of argument. It is nevertheless true that the spirit of capitalism, when it rises above mere managerialism, is consistent with the Puritan ethic that Weber described. At a minimum, even if the Protestants of New England did not actually give birth to the spirit of capitalism, the spirit of capitalism may rightly be said to have profound affinities with the Protestant ethic.

Two more surprises lie in store. First, the higher economic reason of which I speak, whose distinguishing feature is the rejection of a basic axiom of rational choice theory, turns out to coincide with the coordination of economic activity by means of the future that we considered earlier. Both provide a stable basis for promises and contracts, while at the same time causing the paradoxes associated with threats and deterrence to disappear; and in connecting the present with the future, they make it possible to reconcile the ethical foundations of trust with rationality. The second surprise is that this higher reason inescapably involves faith. What matters above all is whether it is good faith or bad faith. When bad faith prevails, crisis and the rationality of rational choice theory gain the upper hand, and Economy's capacity for self-transcendence is destroyed.

The line of inquiry to which I now turn will lead away from history and religious anthropology and plunge us into logic and metaphysics, with a bit of cognitive philosophy and phenomenology thrown in for good measure. I will have proved my point if I can show that these two sets of arguments link up with each other.

Choosing One's Predestination

In Max Weber's account, the Calvinist choice proceeds from a refusal to obey the command of logic, which in this case seems to amount to nothing more than common sense. Very often it happens that I have a choice between several possible courses of action, for instance, whether or not to wear a hat when I leave home in the morning. Although my preference *may* depend on the state of a parameter that is unknown to me when I make my decision (for instance, whether it's going to rain today or not), suppose that in this particular case my decision does *not* depend on it: I prefer to wear my hat whether it's going to rain or not. Does it matter that I do not know whether it's going to rain? Common sense says no. I prefer to wear my hat, period—and if I am rational, I choose to do what I prefer to do. I make my choice without giving any further thought to the matter. The ordinary Calvinist has no idea whether God's eternal decree places him among the blessed or the damned. But since he believes that nothing he may do in this vale of tears will in any way change God's decree, what reason is there to go to the time and trouble (in the event, a very considerable amount of time and trouble) of determining which of these two fates is his? Whether he is damned or blessed won't alter his fate in the least. By parity of reasoning, to revert to our earlier example, why should a person be willing to do whatever it takes to know whether he is suffering from an incurable disease? It is perfectly rational to decline to bear the costs (as an economist would think of them) of time and effort in order to obtain information that will do him no good in the end. A good Calvinist logician is therefore someone who does not care in the least about moral law. This is what Weber means by fatalism: not a sur-render to fate, but the most rational course of action available to a free agent confronted with a quite particular situation, namely, the matter of his own predestination. But Weber finds very few such Calvinists. The great majority of Puritans, he says, *rejected* this rational sort of fatalism.

The theory of rational choice, in analyzing the logic of individual choice in the economic sphere (which it imagines to coincide with the world as a whole, including death itself, as we saw in the last chapter), takes this sort of logical fatalism so seriously that it has elevated it to the status of an axiom. We have already met with it under the name of the strategic dominance principle, but it is also known as the sure thing principle.[25] By way of illustra-tion—and rather than rely, as every economist in the world still does today, on a tiresomely familiar academic fable, the prisoner's dilemma—let us consider the following passage from a famous eighteenth-century novel, *Les liaisons dangereuses*.

In her letter of 4 December 17— to the Vicomte de Valmont, the Mar-quise de Merteuil writes this:

Let's examine the matter: why all this fuss? You found Danceny at my place and you didn't like it? Fine! But what conclusions could you draw from that? Either that, as I said, it was coincidence or else it was deliberate, as I didn't say. In the first case, your letter is unfair; in the second case, it's ridiculous. What was the point of writing? But you're jealous and *jealous people are incapable of reasoning properly.* Very well: I'll do the reasoning for you.

Either you've got a rival or you haven't. If you do have one, you need to make yourself agreeable [in order to be preferred]; if you haven't got one, you still need to be agreeable, to avoid acquiring one. So in either case, you've got to behave in the same way; then why plague yourself? And in particular, why plague me? Have you lost the art of being the most amiable of men? Have you lost confidence in your all-conquering ways? Come now, Vicomte, you're being less than fair to yourself![26]

According to Merteuil, Valmont has a choice between two strategies: either to go on making a show of his jealousy, complaining, making no attempt to hide his resentment, behaving, in short, like a common cuckold; or to make every attempt to please, to prove that his mastery of the arts of seduction is undiminished. Valmont's best course of action (still according to Merteuil) is to choose the second strategy: whether he has been supplanted by a rival or not, it is in his interest, she says, to make himself agreeable. The truth of the matter is unknown to Valmont—he is racked by doubt. The second strategy, Merteuil assures him, leaves no room for doubt, and therefore gives no reason for worry. A rational choice theorist would say that Valmont's uncertainty about his situation entails no uncertainty about which decision is the right one, for it is independent of the situation. In that case the best decision amounts, by definition, to a dominant strategy.

The Marquise de Merteuil's reasoning brings out the apparently implacable logic of *this* logic in a most striking way. But no less forcefully does it expose its limits. Poor Valmont is dying to know! He wants to know if his mistress has cheated on him with young Danceny or not. And he is prepared to pay a high price to find out: in his reply later that same day, Valmont offers Merteuil a choice between peace and war—and she chooses war![27]

Despite its apparently indisputable correctness from the logical point of view, the strategic dominance principle is suspect from the psychological

point of view. What is more—and still more disturbingly, when you stop to
think about it—it is suspect from the point of view of the logic itself. To see
why this should be so, consider what makes the principle appear to be obviously true. Rationality is identified by the economist with a maximization
principle: every agent, whether he is a businessman, a banker, or a consumer,
is supposed to act in such a way as to enlarge a certain magnitude as far as
possible—a quantity of revenue, or profit, or utility, or satisfaction, or whatever it may be. But what does this principle recommend when two criteria
come into conflict with each other? Suppose, for example, that a teacher has
to rank the performance of two pupils, John and Peter, on two sets of tests,
one involving scientific subjects, the other literary subjects. Let us suppose
further that John has better grades than Peter in *each* of the various subjects.
Finally, let us suppose that the weighting coefficients to be assigned to these
various subjects have not yet been decided. This poses no problem in the
present case since, whatever the set of coefficients may be, it is clear that John
must be ranked ahead of Peter; there is no need to wait until the coefficients
have been assigned in order to be sure of this. The presumptively tautological
character of this state of affairs is often illustrated in textbooks by the maxim
that it is better to be handsome and rich than ugly and poor: one does not
have to weigh beauty against wealth in order to be sure it is better to be handsome and rich.

There is nevertheless one case where everyone will admit that the appearance of tautology is due only to a sort of framing effect, namely, where the
choice that is actually made has a causal impact on the parameters that define
the situation of the person who chooses. In that case, the defining property
of a dominant strategy—that this particular option is better than any other,
whatever the situation of the person who chooses may be—loses all meaning,
since the option causally determines the situation. Suppose that Mary likes
to smoke and that she knows this habit is likely to cause lung cancer. On
the one hand, all other things being equal, she would rather smoke than not
smoke; on the other hand, all other things being equal, she would rather not
contract lung cancer. Relying on the principle of strategic dominance, it is
possible to show—falsely, as we shall see—that it is rational for Mary to continue to smoke. The argument runs as follows. Mary does not know whether
she is going to contract lung cancer or not. This does not matter, however,
since if she is going to contract lung cancer she prefers to go on smoking;

and this is also what she prefers to do if it has been foreordained that she will not contract lung cancer. Continuing to smoke is therefore Mary's dominant strategy. What credit should we attach to this argument? None at all, obviously, because it neglects to take into account the causal relation between what Mary decides to do and whether or not she will contract lung cancer. It is precisely this causal relation that rules out the possibility that Mary continues to smoke and does not contract lung cancer.[28]

What would happen if the link between one's options and the parameters of one's situation were counterfactual, though not causal? I maintain that the demonstration I have just given would not be affected in the least, and that the argument from strategic dominance would once again collapse. For economists and rational choice theorists this question never arises since, wittingly or not, they subscribe to the causalist hypothesis. The very possibility of economic reason nevertheless turns on the answer one gives to just this question. A legendary thought experiment will make it clear why.

In the late 1960s, a quantum physicist named William Newcomb invented a formidable paradox that philosophers have argued about ever since and never satisfactorily resolved.[29] There is no reason to think that it is a false paradox, one of those conundrums that, once suitably reformulated, vanishes like the early morning fog. No, it is a true paradox, one that takes us straight to the heart of perhaps the most perplexing enigma of all: how human beings can act freely in a world that is nonetheless causally determined through and through by blind, subjectless processes. Not the least of the virtues of this paradox, from my point of view at any rate, is that it will allow us to recapitulate in an astonishingly concise way the entire argument I have been making in this chapter.

Imagine an agent who is presented with two boxes. One of them is transparent, and visibly contains a thousand dollars; the other is opaque, and, he is told, may contain either a million dollars or nothing at all. The agent is then given a choice between two strategies:

S1. Taking what is in the opaque box alone; and
S2. Taking what is in both boxes.

At the moment when the choice is explained to the agent, a being who has the power to predict the agent's choices will already have placed a million dollars in the opaque box *if and only if* he has predicted that the agent will choose S1. The agent knows this, and, what is more, he has total confidence in the predictive abilities of the predictor. What should he do?

One's first reaction is to say that the agent should choose S1. The predictor will have predicted this choice, and so the agent will have a million dollars. If he were to choose S2 he would have only a thousand dollars—the thousand dollars he sees in the transparent box, while the opaque box would remain empty. The paradox arises from the fact that another way of looking at the matter seems equally persuasive, although it leads to the opposite conclusion. When the agent makes his choice, *either there are or there are not* a million dollars in the opaque box: in taking what is in both boxes, he stands to win a thousand dollars more in either case than if he were to take only what is in the opaque box. S2 is therefore the dominant strategy.

Cognitive psychologists have conducted laboratory experiments showing that the broad stratum of ordinary people (to paraphrase Max Weber)—roughly 75% of the subjects tested—make the choice S1, in violation of the strategic dominance principle.[30] These ordinary people can each claim one million dollars. The remarkable thing is that virtually all professional philosophers, game theorists, and other experts in so-called rational choice choose S2 on the ground that it is the dominant strategy. These experts can each claim a thousand dollars—and also, as a sort of consolation prize, the certainty of being right.

They may be right, but their reward is risibly small by comparison with the amount won by all those ordinary people who, contrary to reason (as the experts define it), *deliberately refuse* to see the obviousness of the dominant strategy. One is tempted to say that Newcomb's problem is worded in such a way that it rewards agents who act irrationally—in which case it would be rational to act irrationally. But this would make no sense unless there were some other criterion of economic rationality than simply maximizing one's gains over a range of possible choices. The difficulty cannot be escaped so easily. What makes Newcomb's problem seem so intractable is that it pits reason against itself.

The incentive to behave irrationally—the million dollars that one assumes to be hidden inside a black box—is manifestly the equivalent of eternal salvation in Max Weber's problem. Indeed, the similarity between the two problems is unmistakable. Anyone who reasons "logically" and chooses

S2 because it is the dominant strategy is a fatalist in Weber's sense: he believes that the opaque box is empty; that, in other words, he is numbered among the damned. The Calvinist, by contrast, is willing to bear a cost in the form of a sacrifice: total commitment to a secular vocation and the unremitting toil this involves in order to be sure of being among the elect, in the one case; foregoing the chance of having the thousand dollars in the transparent box in order to be sure that the opaque box contains a million dollars, in the other. But were not the Lutherans right, then, to complain that the Calvinist, in doing this, mistakes the sign for the thing and imagines, absurdly, that he is able to influence the nature of his predestination?

The interest of Newcomb's problem arises from the fact that it replaces the causal determinism of predestination by another form of determinism that might be called predictive determinism. The question of whether determinism and free will are compatible thus assumes the following form: if an omniscient predictor were to predict that I will take such-and-such an action at instant t, am I free at t not to take this action? Assuming that we are dealing with a human predictor, the matter seems to be settled. In the event that someone who knows me to be an honest person predicts with certainty that I will repay a debt that is soon to come due, which I do in fact then repay, my freedom to act otherwise will have in no way been reduced or compromised. But what if we are dealing with a divine predictor? The "being" who is assumed to intervene in Newcomb's problem is the God of theistic philosophers and rational theologians. His omniscience is, by definition, "essential." This means that if I were to act otherwise than I am about to act, or if I had acted otherwise than I did, God would have foreseen this—in the same way that He foresaw what I did, or what I am about to do, in the world as it actually is. God, in other words, is omniscient in all possible worlds. Economic theory, which is unaware that it is itself a species of theology, has unwittingly made equivalent assumptions: the assumption of perfect foresight, the theory of rational expectations, and so on. This is why economic models constantly encounter Newcomb's problem in one form or another: they are predisposed to do so. Such problems can only arise if there are predictors who do not limit themselves to merely predicting the future, but who change the world as a consequence of their predictions. In theology, this is the definition of providential God, a God who intervenes in human affairs. In economics, all agents are called upon to exercise the same power. It is, one might say, their vocation.

The reasoning of the experimental subject who chooses to take only what is in the opaque box (that is, the subject who makes the Calvinist's choice) amounts to a defense of free choice in the face of a divine predictor. In making this choice, he says, in effect, I expect to find the million dollars in the box. If I were to take what is in both boxes, the million dollars would not be in the opaque box, and I would be left with only the one thousand dollars in the transparent box. In considering himself to be free to choose, and by virtue of exactly this attitude, the subject modifies a definite fact of the past. In Max Weber's problem, the same choice endows the Calvinist with the ability to choose his predestination. But surely this is going too far, no? Isn't the power of acting upon the past, the past that determines who we are, contrary to the laws of physics since it violates a fundamental principle, the irreversibility of time? That would indeed be true if it were understood to be a causal power. There is nothing I can do now or in the future that will cause the wounding words I uttered in a fit of anger, for example, words that have forever alienated someone I love, not to have been uttered. (Only her forgiveness could redeem my sin—but that is another story.) A much less unlikely power is enough to guarantee my freedom: a *counterfactual* power over the past. If I had done this, the past would have been thus-and-such; if I had done otherwise, the past would have been different. When my daughter claims that, had she delayed her trip from Rio to Paris by a day, the crash would not have taken place that day, she is implicitly affirming the existence of such a counterfactual power. Her claim is deducible from the following two-part proposition: a lucky star determines my own intentional choices as well as the blind chain of events that leads to the crash of a plane; and this common cause operates by eliminating from the list of possible worlds all those worlds in which I take the plane and it crashes into the sea.[31]

One cannot act causally on the past. Nevertheless one may act counterfactually on it. What I call the causalist hypothesis holds that counterfactual independence obtains between two variables if and only if they are causally independent of each other. The very fact that a counterfactual power over the past can reasonably be asserted to exist demonstrates that the causalist hypothesis is not universally valid. And yet it is on the causalist hypothesis that the obviousness—the false obviousness, if I am right—of the strategic dominance principle rests.

I remarked earlier that many scientists are unwilling to accept Popper's claim that every science is erected on the basis of a metaphysics of one sort or another. Economists, who as practitioners of a "soft" science feel a certain sense of inferiority, have shown still greater resistance to this idea, even though economic theory is filled to the point of overflowing with assumptions about human behavior, freedom of choice and causal determinism, and the relation between the past, present, and future for which no positivist science could provide empirical evidence. If an economist were to read this chapter, he might wonder what a God who is omniscient in all possible worlds could possibly have to do with economics. I should reply to him as Laplace replied to Napoleon, when Napoleon inquired about God's place in his vision of the world—a vision no less theological than that of rational theology, for it is founded on an absolute causal determinism: "Sire, I have no need of that hypothesis." We have already encountered a type of behavior that makes no appeal to divine intervention, that assumes nothing more than the willingness of human beings to try to live together as best they can, and that exhibits all of the paradoxical features I have just discussed, namely, coordination by means of the future. We saw that it is the very thing a truly moral and political economy cannot do without if it is to flourish. Now, finally, we are in a position to understand why this should be so. For now we can see that the solution to Weber's paradox has been hiding in plain sight the whole time: economic reason rests on a Calvinist type of choice (whether or not the Puritans of New England actually made this choice is unimportant), which consists in deliberately rejecting the strategic dominance principle, notwithstanding that this principle is one of the pillars of the economic theory of rational choice.

If it is assumed that individual choices are freely made, then postulating an omniscient predictor in all possible worlds and treating the future as *fixed* (which is to say, as counterfactually—though not causally—independent of present actions) are equivalent propositions. Once I act as I do, this action determines the predictor's prediction, not causally but counterfactually. In other words, if I had acted otherwise the predictor's prediction would have been different—and it is this prediction that causally determines my action at the same time. At the very moment that I act I make my action necessary, so that every other action simultaneously would have been impossible. This was not true, however, before I acted: I could then have acted otherwise than I did since, having not yet acted, what causally determines my action was not yet counterfactually determined. This loop between the future and the past, on which I dwelt at such great length earlier, can now be represented in a somewhat different, though complementary way (figure 2).

Under coordination by means of the future, in other words, the future counterfactually determines the past, which in turn causally determines it. The future is fixed, but its necessity exists only in retrospect.

I call this temporal metaphysics "projected time," an allusion to the philosophy of Jean-Paul Sartre. As in this philosophy, but perhaps even more so in that of Sartre's teacher, Henri Bergson, the basic elements of standard modal logic—possibility, contingency, necessity, impossibility—behave strangely. The truth-value of propositions in which they figure is not eternal; it depends instead on when they are stated. In projected time, as I say, necessity is retrospective: before I act, it was not necessary that I act as I do; once I have acted, *it will always have been true* that I could not have acted otherwise than I did.[32] The same may be said of events that do not depend on what I do. Once they have occurred, it is true that it was written down on the scroll of eternity, foreordained, that they had to occur; but before they occur, it is not true that they necessarily had to occur. No one should suppose for a moment that this is simply the ranting of a deranged philosopher. The temporal metaphysics I have sketched here is the metaphysics of the ordinary person and, in particular, of the ordinary person in most rural parts of the world.[33] Think, for example, of misfortune: it is when misfortune occurs, and not before, that its occurrence appears to have been forever decreed by an implacable destiny. Weber's "broad stratum of ordinary believers," when they make the Calvinist's choice, spontaneously situate themselves in projected time in the same fashion.

Nor can this metaphysics be accused of fatalism. Exactly the opposite is true, in fact. However much it may appear that individuals are creatures of destiny, they are nonetheless the ones who choose their destiny. Weber's Puritans are predestined—but they pay a high price for being predestined to eternal salvation.

Recall the argument I developed earlier, in the second chapter, in connection with self-transcendence and the concept of coordination by means of the future. The condition that must be satisfied if a loop between past and future is to close on itself is a demanding one. It is satisfied only by a restricted set of sequences of events and actions conforming to a maxim, or

Figure 2. Coordination by Means of the Future

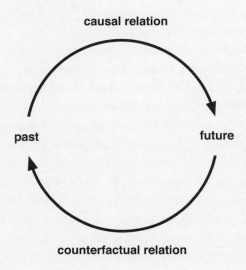

categorical imperative, that can now be restated thus: Act always in such a way that your action would remain causally possible in the event it were to be anticipated by a predictor whose omniscience is essential, that is, true in all possible worlds. Making a promise that one has no intention of keeping when the time comes, for example, is automatically ruled out. The implication of this maxim is fundamental. In neoclassical economics, as we saw earlier, agents who are "rational" in the sense given this term by rational choice theory, which holds the principle of strategic dominance sacred, are unable to trust each other or to keep their promises. This is why economics needs the helping hand of what it calls ethics if economic life is to be possible at all, which is to say a world in which people are animated by a conception of the future that is sufficiently optimistic to be desirable and sufficiently credible to give rise to actions that will bring about its own realization. If I have not misinterpreted Weber, economic reason, in defending freedom against determinism in its strongest imaginable form (and so deliberately rejecting the causalist hypothesis), *by itself* implies an ethics of promising and trusting. Economic reason can therefore be said to form the basis of a genuinely political and moral economy.[34]

The Calvinist's Choice and the Faith of Bad Faith

The Calvinist's choice is the example that is most frequently chosen, as it happens, by American philosophers who seek to illustrate what they call self-deception. This same concept, as we saw at the very beginning, is found under the name of self-deceit in the work of an eighteenth-century moral philosopher who had not yet invented economics, Adam Smith. By virtue of a paradox that lies at the heart of self-deception, the challenge it presents is now appreciated by philosophers working in numerous branches of the analytic tradition: philosophy of mind (closely associated with research in cognitive science), philosophy of language, philosophy of action, and moral and political philosophy. My own view is that Weber's problem would have been dealt with more incisively if the Continental tradition, and particularly phenomenology of mind, had taken an interest in it: Sartre rather than Donald Davidson, the concept of bad faith (*mauvaise foi*) rather than self-deception.[35] But it is not too late to do make a start in this direction.

Davidson, it is by no means irrelevant to note in this connection, began his career as a rational choice theorist. Later, as a convinced rationalist who had in the meantime become a leading figure in the analytic philosophy of action, he took a particular interest in two forms of irrationality that he found deeply puzzling: self-deception and weakness of the will (*akrasia*). In the latter case, a person sees the right thing to do and does the opposite; in the former, he lies to himself. Now, Davidson did not himself believe that it is possible to lie to oneself, on account of a well-known paradox that Sartre had to confront as well, namely, that one cannot lie without knowing that one is lying. How, then, could anyone be the victim of his own lie, since he knows that he is lying to himself?

Davidson's solution, which all analytic philosophers have commented upon, whether to praise it or to condemn it, proceeds by means of an argument from belief. Taking an example that seems to have preoccupied him personally at the time, of a man embarrassed by his advancing baldness who manages by various cosmetic and, above all, psychological expedients to deny the obvious (more to himself than to others), Donaldson described the mental state of such a man thus: he believes two things at once, both that he is bald *and* that he is not bald; he must find a way to overlook the fact that he holds the first belief, because he wishes to "see" only the second; and yet it is *because* he holds the first belief that a psychological mechanism of wishful thinking is activated and he begins to entertain the second. The first belief, in other words, is the cause of the second, though evidently without being the reason for it, for it contradicts the second belief.[36]

Note that Davidson refuses not only to treat self-deception in terms of lying. He also rejects Sartre's solution, that such a man simultaneously believes something and does not believe it—for in that case, according to Davidson, it is the philosopher who would be guilty of inconsistency and not the person whose situation he is considering! Sartrians have good grounds for taking issue with this view, but Davidson's description has the virtue of psychological parsimony. By allowing two contradictory beliefs to coexist in the mind of a single person, Davidson seeks to partition the mind in such a way as to avoid a collision between irreconcilable claims about reality. Yet we are not in Freud's world here. There is no need to claim that one or the other of these mental compartments is the seat of the unconscious.[37]

The transposition of this argument to the analysis of the Calvinist's choice is straightforward. Furthermore, it is supported by Weber's own words, for he says that Calvinism produced "self-confident 'saints.'"[38] One may therefore assert the following two propositions:

(1) Calvinists believe that they achieve salvation themselves by choosing to acquire the signs of grace.
(2) Calvinists believe that they do not achieve salvation themselves.

These propositions express contradictory beliefs. Let us assume that Calvinists manage to conceal (1) from themselves because they wish to believe (2), that is, that that they have been elected by God. If we assume furthermore that the first belief is the *cause* of the second, without, of course, constituting a reason for it, then we obtain a pure case of self-deception in Davidson's sense.

There can be no objection, certainly not on empirical grounds, to this way of characterizing the Calvinist's choice. Twenty years ago Amos Tversky carried out an impressive series of experiments in which he placed subjects in situations having the same logical structure as Weber's paradox. Remarkably, not only did the great majority of subjects make the Calvinist's choice, they also denied (to the experimenter, and probably also to themselves) having *intentionally* made this choice in order to reassure themselves as to their membership among the elect.[39] I would like simply to propose another way of interpreting the paradox that has the effect of bringing out the *rationality* of the Calvinist's choice. We have already considered this alternate view, as it happens, but it will be helpful to briefly examine it once more using the conceptual tools of analytic philosophy of mind, without pausing here to challenge the manner in which this philosophy treats beliefs.

The second interpretation attributes to Calvinists the two following beliefs, which are not (or at least are not necessarily) incompatible:

(3) Calvinists believe that they do not achieve salvation themselves, because they believe that they have been elected by God.

(4) Calvinists believe that they were free to make the contrary choice (idleness—the "fatalistic" choice) when they acted (choosing to put their faith to the test of earthly works).

On the first interpretation, proposition (2) is where the irrationality comes in: Calvinists are attached to the belief that they are not responsible for their own salvation because, deep down, they know that they *have* actively sought to acquire the signs of their election and they wish to conceal this truth from themselves. On the second interpretation, however, the reason Calvinists believe they do not ensure their own salvation is simply that they take seriously the facts of the matter as it has been presented to them and as they have become accustomed to think about it: God, not man, has ordained their salvation. They are therefore confronted with a seemingly insurmountable obstacle: they have to consider it not inconsistent to believe both that God has chosen for them (proposition (3)) and that they are free to choose themselves (proposition (4)). In other words, in order for them (and for us) to be able to take Weber's problem seriously, one must convince oneself that it is reasonable to be a *compatibilist*—that it is reasonable to believe in the compatibility of determinism (in this case, causal determinism) and free will. The way out from this impasse, I believe, is to be found in Sartrian phenomenology. It is remarkable that Sartre's conception of what he calls bad faith in *Being and Nothingness* (1943), should echo this second interpretation of the Calvinist choice, which aims at establishing the rationality of the Calvinist's choice within an analytic framework. This does not mean, however, that there are not considerable differences between the two approaches.

From a compatibilist perspective, in which freedom holds its own with determinism, it becomes possible actually to choose one's own predestination. On Sartre's view of the matter, freedom is so absolute that it extends even to the choice of a past. Thus one encounters a sentence in *Being and Nothingness* such as this: "For us to 'have' a past, we must perpetuate its existence by the very act of projecting ourselves into the future: we do not receive our past; but the necessity of our contingency implies that *we cannot not choose it*."[40] Or this one, which leaves even the few analytic philosophers who approach Sartre with sympathy and an open mind at a loss: "Thus, in a certain sense, I choose to be born."[41] Alain Renaut has shown that this idea has its roots in Heidegger's analysis of the historicity of "human-reality" (*Dasein*).[42] For Heidegger, Renaut observes, human-reality is "'historical above all else' inasmuch as its essential property is *choosing* what appears to it in some way as *fate*."[43] In other words, "What we call 'fate' is the 'resoluteness' (*Entschlossenheit*) of 'human-reality.'"[44] In Sartre this becomes: "To be finite is to *choose oneself*, that is, to reveal to oneself what one is by projecting oneself into one possible to the exclusion of all others."[45]

It is startling to see how easily the argument that leads to the perfect rationality of the Calvinist's choice can be re-created by taking in turn, one after the other, the propositions found in *Being and Nothingness* about the freedom to choose oneself by projecting oneself into the future and, by virtue of just this, choosing one's fate. One cannot help but be reminded of Economy, which is pulled forward by a future that it has cast beyond itself—what we have been calling coordination by means of the future. Just as "when Adam took the apple, it would have been *possible* for him not to take it,"[46] so too, when the Calvinist makes his choice, it would have been possible for him to make the opposite choice. Just as Adam would then have been another Adam, so too the Calvinist would have been another Calvinist: instead of having been saved, he would have been damned.

Sartre takes the example of Adam and the apple in order to set himself apart from Leibniz. For Leibniz, Adam's essence is not chosen by Adam, but by God. His freedom is therefore only an illusion. For Sartre, by contrast, Adam's existence precedes his essence. "It is therefore the future, and not the past, that reveals his *identity* to him: he chooses to discover what he is through the ends toward which he projects himself."[47] The free Calvinist, in the interpretation that reveals the rationality of his choice, is at once Leibnizian and Sartrian. His essence determines his existence, but, since he has the freedom of choosing his existence, he has the freedom of choosing his essence as well. He has, literally, the power to choose his predestination. But, as I say, this power is not causal; otherwise causality would be supposed, nonsensically, to run contrary to the arrow of time. It is instead a *counterfactual* power over the past. To say this much makes it clear that the whole metaphysical edifice I have just described rests on a deliberate rejection of the causalist hypothesis.

The individual, knowing himself to be free, reasons in the following way. If I were to decide to do this, rather than the opposite, my action would be the *sign* that I am in a certain world, with its own past, with its own determining features, with the distinctive essence that this world reserves for me. If I were to decide to act otherwise, then I would be in another world and my essence would be different. It is not that my action causally determines the world that is mine; it *reveals* it. And yet, since I am both free *and* rational, my choice must satisfy what mathematicians call an extremum principle: it maximizes my utility, my pleasure, my happiness, or what have you—it hardly matters which in this case, for it will readily be admitted that the Calvinist prefers eternal salvation to eternal damnation, even if this salvation is obtained at the price of sentencing oneself to a life of hard labor. I therefore choose to acquire the signs of my salvation, without thereby considering that I cause my salvation in this way, by purchasing it through works.

The compatibilism on which the Calvinist's choice rests produces the peculiar temporality that I have called projected time. It is the temporality peculiar to someone who carries out a plan that he has given to himself to carry out. He is, in other words, both author and actor: the scenario has already been written when he acts, but since he is free, he can pull himself up to the level where the scenario can be read, as it were, and exert upon it the counterfactual power of which I speak. The sort of bootstrapping that characterizes projected time therefore makes it a kind of ethical time as well, which is to say a process by which a person manages to transcend his own individuality and project himself into a universal.

This self-transcendence can also be detected in Sartre, but in order to see it one must circle back to his theory of consciousness, which is wholly opposed to the theory advanced by analytic philosophy (and by the cognitive science that underlies this philosophy). As a successor to the phenomenological tradition inaugurated by Edmund Husserl, Sartre regards consciousness not as a state, but as an evanescent process that constantly slips away from us, never for a moment coinciding with itself, instead producing within itself the self-transcendence, the exteriority of the self in relation to itself that Husserl called transcendence-within-immanence. At the beginning of *Being and Nothingness*, Sartre poses the question: "What sort of being must man be, to be capable of bad faith?"[48] He answers: "Bad faith can only exist when human reality . . . is what it is not and is not what it is."[49] And again: "For bad faith to be possible, sincerity itself must be bad faith."[50] By this he means that bad faith ultimately has the same structure of self-transcendence, of transcendence-within-immanence, as consciousness itself. This is why Sartre holds that the structure of consciousness is revealed most directly through a transcendental analysis of the conditions under which bad faith is possible. It is also, unfortunately, why bad faith as he understands it turns out to be wholly disconnected from the consciousness of others. Sartre's solipsism is no less complete than that of analytic philosophers of mind. Bad faith fits consciousness like a glove—so snugly, in fact, that it may be wondered whether the glove can be taken off and whether "authenticity" can ever be achieved.

Sartre's theory of belief is part of his theory of consciousness. In the third part of the chapter on bad faith, entitled "The 'Faith' of Bad Faith," one finds a raft of brilliant insights that, to the positivist way of thinking, make no sense whatsoever. "Belief," Sartre says, "is a being that calls its own being into question, that can realize itself only through its [own] destruction, that can manifest itself to itself only by denying itself; it is a being for which to be is to appear, and to appear is to deny oneself. Believing is not believing."[51] And there is this: "To believe is to know that one believes, and to know that one believes is no longer to believe. Thus believing is no longer believing, because that is only believing."[52] To say that "belief becomes non-belief"[53] permits Sartre to maintain that a person of bad faith both believes and does not believe in a state of affairs that he finds embarrassing (going bald, for example)—something that Davidson considers an absurdity.

Sartre's great virtue, it has been said, was to have converted Husserl's theory of consciousness into a philosophy of freedom. In each case we are faced with the same logical structure of self-transcendence. It is precisely the resemblance of this logic to the logic of the Calvinist's choice that allows us to make sense of it. What Renaut sees as a tension in Sartre's analysis of freedom, between Spinoza's concept of acquiescence to a prior necessity and Kant's model of absolute autonomy,[54] is mirrored by the Calvinist's choice, in which the individual's acquiescence in fate coexists with his own making of this same fate. The fact that bad faith is faith, which is to say belief, Sartre says, is exactly what distinguishes it from lying. "How can we believe, in bad faith," he asks, "in concepts that we create expressly in order to persuade ourselves?"—a rhetorical question that agrees perfectly with the Calvinist's choice. Immediately he draws the conclusion: "A belief formed in bad faith must itself be an act of bad faith."[55] With regard to the means employed to persuade oneself—and here, obviously, one thinks of the Calvinist's *action*, carried out *in order* to believe—he adds: "To admit to myself that I resorted to these means in bad faith would have been cynicism; to believe that I was innocent in resorting to them would have been sincerity."[56] Sartre is searching here for an improbable intermediate position, but its consistency is once again perfectly illustrated by the choice made by the Calvinist, who believes himself to be neither wholly innocent in the matter of his election nor wholly responsible for it. It is this choice, I say, that gives birth to economic reason.

"Faith," Sartre says, "is decision."[57] And again, in connection with those affinities between two persons that are called *elective* affinities: "I believe that my friend Pierre considers me his friend. . . . I *believe it*; that is, . . . I decide to believe it and hold fast to this decision; in short, I behave as though I were certain of it."[58] A better definition of the Calvinist's faith could hardly be imagined. The similarity between the two extends even to Sartre's use of the French word *évidence*, meaning "obviousness," to which he gives almost the sense of its English counterpart: a manifestation, a sign or symptom. The kind of obviousness that is expressed by bad faith, Sartre says, is "*unpersuasive* obviousness."[59] The minority of rational choice theorists who defend the rationality of the Calvinist's choice, as I do, call their position "evidentialist"—precisely because the choice is made with a view to acquiring for oneself, at great personal cost, the outward *signs* of election.

The parallel between the Calvinist's faith and the faith of Sartre's bad faith nevertheless should not be pushed too far. Evidentialists are led to conclude that the Calvinist's choice is rational because they assume a strict form of determinism. The Calvinist embraces this determinism, to be sure, but it nonetheless remains wholly external to him. Sartre, on the other hand, is resolved not to abandon the postulate enunciated at the outset of his analysis of bad faith: "Bad faith does not come to human reality from outside."[60] One may wonder whether this postulate does not commit him to a theory of bad faith (and consciousness) every bit as solipsistic as the theory of self-deception put forward by analytic philosophers. Is it really possible to deceive oneself all alone, without the negative cooperation of others? I began this book by recalling that Adam Smith looked upon Economy as a vast theater in which society deludes itself. Could it be that Sartre was a mainstream economic theorist without knowing it, and despite knowing rather little about economic life? That Adam Smith, a moralistic Scottish Puritan, was a better judge of human nature than the founder of French existentialism? If these things are so, then our system of values will clearly need to be reformed.

The Lie of Individualism

The rejection of the causalist hypothesis is a necessary, but not a sufficient, condition of economic reason in Max Weber's sense—the kind of reason that allows Economy, with the impetus provided by political transcendence, to pull itself out of the morass of managerialism and assume its rightful place as a moral and political economy. The structure of self-transcendence is what makes this form of bootstrapping possible, but gives no assurance that it will in fact take place. We have already seen what happens when self-transcendence goes wrong, in the form of market panic, for example, or of Keynesian deflation.

The best way of understanding bad faith is to think of it as a story that one tells oneself about oneself. There is no self-deception without fiction. This may be why literature has always been very closely associated with bad faith, either because it often depicts bad faith or because it is itself composed in bad faith—or both. By way of conclusion I should like to consider one of the most famous and most influential novels of the twentieth century, Albert Camus's *The Stranger*.

The extraordinary reputation this novel has enjoyed since its publication seventy years ago, and enjoys still among young people today, is well known. Even so, no one of good faith can fail to have had a strange feeling, bordering on unease, on reading *The Stranger* for the first time. Sartre himself, in a very penetrating piece of criticism, sought to uncover the literary and philosophical technique by which Camus was able to produce this feeling in his readers. The consciousness of the central character, the stranger, Meursault, is made transparent to us, but the transparency is only partial: things happen, but they seem to make no sense. Sartre says of the author: "*He lies*—like every artist—because he claims to reconstitute raw experience and because he cunningly separates out all the meaningful relationships that are a part of it."[61] It is by no means incidental that Sartre should go on at once to place this insight in the service of what he imagines to be a lethal attack against Anglo-American empiricism and, in particular, analytic philosophy, which he accuses of raising the same technique to the rank of philosophical method: "The universe of the absurd man is the analytic world of the neorealists."[62]

No one, to my knowledge, has had either the lucidity or the courage to say, in purely human terms, what either Meursault's lie or the lie of his creator amounts to—no one with the exception of René Girard, in an essay that appeared some twenty years after Camus's book came out and that did much to establish his reputation as a literary critic.[63] Meursault, it will be recalled, is a colorless person, in no way remarkable. His only distractions are drinking café au lait in the morning and long Sunday afternoons spent looking through the louvered shutters of his apartment window at the people passing by in the street below. In the meantime he carries on a sexual relationship that seems to hold no interest for him. Inexplicably, in the middle of the novel, Meursault kills an Arab. He ends up on the scaffold. Not only critics, but Camus himself, had said over and over again that it was not for this murder that Meursault was sentenced to death; he was punished for his strangeness, his remoteness from society, his marginality—*the fact that he did not cry at his mother's funeral*. What, then, is the meaning of the murder? The critics reply: chance, fate, an accident, an error. But, Girard objects with devastating sarcasm, Camus's novel "does not prove that people who do not cry at their mothers' funerals are likely to be sentenced to death. All the novel proves . . . is that these people will be sentenced to death *if they also happen* to commit involuntary manslaughter, and this *if*, it will be conceded, is a very big one."[64] The murder committed by Meursault has all the properties of a *supplément*, in Derrida's sense of the term: it is useless, for it adds nothing to the fullness of the fate to which Meursault is condemned, and yet at the same time it is indispensable, since without it his fate could not be fulfilled. To deconstruct this paradoxical logic, the reader must understand that Camus's novel suffers from a structural defect that itself is due neither to chance nor to error. This flaw has a logic of its own, the logic of a particular kind of lie—lying to oneself.

Camus makes himself Meursault's accomplice. Meursault is what Girard calls a *boudeur*—a sulker, a sullen loner whose deceitfulness Camus aids and abets. The loner suffers from society's indifference; solitude in an anonymous world is unbearable to him. Thus he makes himself believe that he wishes to be alone and that it is society, jealous of what makes him different from others, that persists in persecuting him, even when his back is against the wall. For this upside-down picture of reality to take hold in the loner's mind, to acquire some measure of plausibility, it must be shared by society. The loner does indeed wish to be alone and marginal, but only so long as others know it. Meursault therefore finds himself in the grip of a familiar paradox: he must communicate to society his refusal to communicate. It can only be resolved by means of an incomprehensible act: he shoots the Arab in a mood of extreme detachment, negligently—inadvertently, one might say, just as a sullen child might burn down a house by setting fire to the curtains. In principle this act should be of no importance, for it adds nothing to his situation in the world: it is Meursault's social marginalization, his difference from his neighbors, that is responsible for the punishment that is suddenly visited upon him, and not the act itself. This is why he commits the act as though he did not commit it. He does not feel any more personal responsibility for it than for an accident, or for something that had been fated to happen. Without this *nonact*, however, the upside-down picture of the world that he has created for himself, the implausible story he has made up and made himself believe, could never come true. Through the act itself he becomes pure *en-soi*, a thing among other things that simply is. Meursault's finger pulling the trigger is the same *thing* as the hand that Sartre imagines a young woman unthinkingly surrendering to an ardent admirer: she "leaves her hand [in his], *without being aware* of leaving it there."[65]

I have just summarized Girard's reading of Camus's story. Our examination of the Calvinist's choice suggests an illuminating connection between the two: Meursault, like the Calvinist, produces his own fate. There are nonetheless two essential differences. The first is that it is no longer a matter of self-election, but of self-exclusion. Meursault's *choice*, to kill the Arab and end up on the scaffold, is the exact converse of the Calvinist who seeks to acquire the signs of his election. In both cases a process of what might be called self-sacralization is at work. But the sacred has two faces, one luminous, the other dark. It is Meursault's fate to embody the second. Sartre sensed this perfectly, writing about Camus's character: "His absurdity nevertheless appears to us as something given, rather than earned: that's just the way he is, and that's that. He will have his moment of illumination on the final page, but he has been living the whole time according to M. Camus's rules. *If the absurd had its own grace, we would have to say that he enjoys grace.*"[66]

And yet Sartre does not go far enough. He seems to be saying that Camus is to Meursault as God is to the Calvinists. But when Sartre speaks of the "moment of illumination" that Meursault will have at the end, he comes much nearer to the truth. In the last sentence of the book, the eternal outsider betrays for the first time a human sentiment, relishing the prospect that a crowd filled with hatred will greet him with cries of loathing and disgust when he mounts the scaffold. It is here, in the view of God as other people, that we find the second difference between Meursault's choice and the Calvinist's choice. Meursault needs other people in order to be able to tell them he has no need of them. However paradoxical this may seem, it is a commonplace of modern individualism—the writer who wishes to be read so that his readers will know they do not matter to him; the media-savvy intellectual who goes on talk shows in order to express his contempt for them; Alceste, in Molière's *The Misanthrope*, who cannot bring himself to leave the stage until he is sure his rivals, the young noblemen competing for Célimène's favors, realize that their company holds no interest for him.

Alain Renaut has brilliantly argued the case that existentialism is an individualism (not, as Sartre famously maintained, a humanism).[67] There are good grounds for comparing Meursault's self-exclusion with the self-proclaimed solitude ("I am all alone") of Antoine Roquentin, in Sartre's *Nausea*, as with that of Dostoyevsky's underground man ("I am alone, and they, they are all"). But it needs to be kept in mind that individualism is a lie. To be sure, not just any lie: it is a collective lie to oneself. Individualism is riddled with bad faith, but in this case it is not Sartre's bad faith, which remains sealed off for the most part inside personal consciousness. The bad faith I am trying to get at, the one from which the modern individual suffers, can be conceived and brought into existence only through what Heidegger called "being-with"—that curious, negative form of collaboration with others.[68]

A society dominated by Economy produces Meursaults by the dozen. Most of them, of course, do not go so far as to commit murder. But human beings have become *strangers* to one another. Others—all those who make up the "hell" that Sartre immortalized—are so many obstacles on the path that every person clears for himself in trying to reach what he takes to be the good life. He is constantly telling others that he does not need them. But he does need them: without them, his words would never be heard. We ourselves are constantly telling other people that they do not exist for us—a paradox of modern life that advanced "communications technologies" permit us to resolve with the greatest of ease.

Today we are all Newcomb's children. Most people have never heard of his problem, yet they are confronted with it all the time. In order for Newcomb's problem to exist, one must attach enormous importance to a particular kind of personal status (being among the elite performers in a given field of endeavor, acting in such a way that some black box or other will not be empty, and so on) that cannot be directly apprehended. We have access only to the *signs* of this status, and in particular to those signs that we detect in others, especially in their gaze—in the same way that the Greeks thought they could know the nature of their *daímōn*, their own personal lot or fate, only by looking at the pupil of another person's eye. Does anyone doubt that we are prepared to pay a very high price so that these signs will be favorable? Think of how many people are willing to *buy* the favorable opinion of others. But isn't this completely irrational? What good is it to have their approval if we know we do not deserve it? And if we know that it is deserved, it matters little or not at all to us that others do not know it. "When a man has bribed all the judges, the most unanimous decision of the court, though it may gain him his law-suit, cannot give him any assurance that he was in the right; and had he carried on his law-suit merely to satisfy himself that he was in the right, he never would have bribed the judges."[69] This apparently commonsensical observation comes from the pen of Adam Smith. It was when Smith realized that his astonishment at this apparently irrational behavior arose from a profound naïveté that he became an economist and wrote *The Wealth of Nations*. He understood the reason why men bribe their fellow men in order to win their praise: when the "higher tribunal" of conscience is silent, or uncertain, only public opinion can furnish standards of excellence and praiseworthiness.[70]

In *The Theory of Moral Sentiments*, Smith describes the struggle between what he calls the impartial spectator (also the "man within") and the flesh-and-blood spectator (the "man without"), constantly prey to worldly desires and passions.[71] It is a struggle between an ideal and a reality: the ideal of a conscience freed once and for all from its origins in social life, and the reality of public opinion in all of its unpredictable volatility. Everyone owes it to himself to read the superb chapter that Smith devotes to the desire of being approved by others, and to the relation between this desire and the desire of being worthy of such approval—which is to say, of being approved by oneself.[72] What Smith would like to show is that, although this second desire is rooted in the first, it may yet acquire a certain autonomy, a relative independence, once conscience has succeeded in raising itself, by an effort of self-transcendence, above the judgment of others, of ordinary spectators. But he does not succeed. In the end it is economic wealth that triumphs. Why? Because wealth is the one thing on which all individual desires converge. In attracting the attention of other people to ourselves—people who stand in exactly the same relation to wealth as we do—wealth becomes the sign of that quality of being that everyone wishes to possess, without ever being certain that he does possess it. The choice of making the accumulation of wealth one's chief aim in life—of assuring oneself that one is worthy because one is wealthy—has the same metaphysical structure as the Calvinist's choice, but not the same value. The immutable and eternal decision of God has been replaced by the unpredictable and capricious judgment of the crowd.

We have therefore exchanged a sublime conception of human purpose and worth for a ridiculous one. These two ideas, having the same paradoxical logic, may be thought of as the positive and negative sides of Economy, proof of its fundamental ambivalence: on the one side, the triumph of freedom over determinism, the capacity of a human community to choose its destiny in lifting itself out of the present, pulling itself forward by means of a future of its own imagining that serves it as a traction point;[73] on the other, the mendacious retreat into a private sphere of selfish consumption, in which one's relationship to others is limited to communicating signs that have been devised expressly to cut off communication. On the one side, faith—a secular faith, what is commonly, but obscurely, called confidence in the future;

on the other, the faith of bad faith. In Sartre, bad faith has the same structure as consciousness, that is, transcendence-within-immanence. In the realm of Economy, the structure of self-transcendence is common to two forms of collective being, two forms of becoming-together: freedom and self-confidence, which allow us to open ourselves up to the future; and self-exclusion, by which we persuade ourselves that every person is a stranger to every other. We have passed from one to the other, from truth to falsehood, from life to death. Nothing prohibits us from hoping that our steps may yet be undone.

The Way Out from Fatalism

Fatalists, in Max Weber's problem, are believers who exercise their freedom of choice by being rational. In doing this they understand rationality in the same way that economists do, and they respect an axiom that economists take to be indispensable, the dominant strategy principle. This sort of freedom leads them to act in a way that makes it clear to them that they are damned and that there is nothing they can do to change this state of affairs. It is the same freedom exercised by people who choose to take what is in both boxes in Newcomb's problem and discover, as they ought to have expected, that the opaque box is empty. A queer sort of freedom, one might say. But it is a queer sort of fatalism as well. As freedom it is odd because it amounts to *choosing* fatalism; as fatalism it is odd because it is the result of a *deliberate* choice.

Fatalism is bound to get a bad press in an individualist society, which sees itself as guided by reason. A society that believes no science of the future is possible because the future cannot be known in advance, but instead is purely the product of human will, will have nothing to do with fatalism. The problem is that the antifatalism such a society urges upon its members is precisely what Weber means by fatalism! It is the fatalism of all those who believe they are free to choose and who always choose the losing strategy, in the name of rationality. It is a simple matter to clear up this latest paradox. Free will, as it is understood by a society that has been bewildered and bamboozled by Economy, is the bastard offspring of what I called earlier a supermarket metaphysics. This vulgar antifatalism—the view that at any moment there is a multitude of options from which to choose, a myriad of paths that may be taken, and from these the best one is invariably chosen—jumps head first into all of the traps that the dominant strategy has set for it. Mutual trust, on this view, is irrational, and only a deus ex machina—"ethics"—can bring it into existence. Mutually advantageous transactions cannot take place, owing to a general mistrust that occludes the temporal horizon and prevents Economy from transcending itself. This mistrust takes the form of a withdrawal into oneself, the same retreat that degenerates into flights of panic and produces the madness of crowds in all its other forms. Deterrence in such a world is powerless to curb aggression among either states or persons, with the result that peace becomes an increasingly scarce commodity.[1] Newcomb's opaque box cannot help but be completely empty for anyone who looks to economic theory for guidance in the matter of rationality.

No sooner had I begun, in a series of earlier books, to investigate the metaphysics of projected time in the particular case where a future catastrophe has been foretold (a problem we examined in chapter 3 of the present book), than I had cause to regret the name I had given to my method of analysis. For the association of projected time with what I called enlightened (or rational) doomsaying gave this metaphysics the appearance of fatalism in the minds of most of my critics. And yet nothing could be further from the truth. Enlightened doomsaying is a form of optimism, and, moreover, one that is founded on reason.

Let me briefly recall the circumstances that led me to develop this line of argument. The main challenge posed by major catastrophes, whether they are moral, natural, industrial, or technological in character, is that their potential victims find it almost impossible to believe that disaster is imminent, even though they have available to them all the information needed to conclude that the worst is very likely, if not actually certain, to happen. It is not owing to a lack of knowledge that people do not act, but to the fact that knowledge is not transformed into belief. This is the obstacle that must be overcome. The method of enlightened doomsaying counsels us to act *as if* a catastrophic occurrence were our fate, but nonetheless a fate that we are free to reject.

Since it is far more difficult to reject a fate than to avoid a calamity, the threat of catastrophe becomes far more credible if it appears to be something that is inevitable. Once its credibility has been established, however, the same threat creates the driving force that mobilizes imagination, intelligence, and resolute determination—all the resources that must be brought to bear if catastrophe is to be prevented. The method I recommend is therefore anything but fatalistic. Its reliance on the metaphysical fiction of fate amounts to a kind of detour in the spirit of Leibniz, who was fond of quoting the old French proverb that often it is necessary to take a step back in order to leap forward (*reculer pour mieux sauter*). In this case one steps back from a weak conception of freedom in order to leap over it and attain true freedom, a freedom that is strong enough to overcome necessity.

The prophet of misfortune proclaims the inevitability of a cataclysm so that it will not occur. The paradox is twofold: not only is fate something that can be chosen, this choice takes the form of a refusal.[2] The prophet of good fortune has an easier task. He announces a desirable and credible fate so that his prediction will be fulfilled. Fate is still the object of a choice in this case, but here choice is a sort of acquiescence. This is not so very different from Spinoza's idea that freedom is the consciousness, or the acceptance, of necessity. In my conception of projected time, the paradox involves a splitting into two that takes place when we allow ourselves to be guided by a future that we ourselves have projected in front of us. In Rousseau's terms, it is in obeying the law we have given to ourselves that we make ourselves free. This freedom corresponds to the self-transcendence of the political domain.

We now find ourselves back where we began, better prepared (or so we must hope) to rehabilitate the prophetic dimension of politics by disentangling it from what I have called economystification, the process by which politics has been made the lackey of economics. It is just this tendency, alas, that is beginning to gather momentum as I write these lines, in November 2011: political leadership in Europe supinely yields to the superior judgment of experts; government by human beings yields to "governance" by things; political reason yields to economic rationality under the wary eye of that monstrous beast known as "the markets."

"The world is now at war with the financial markets," as one cabinet minister recently put it. Nothing more false—indeed, nothing more ridiculous—could be imagined. Consider, by contrast, the words of the famous comic-strip character Pogo Possum: "We have met the enemy and he is us." Pogo was a thousand times more right than the minister. Modern societies, entirely dominated by Economy, are in grave and imminent danger of perishing from an evil that they themselves have produced. Politicians, no matter that every last one of them is bewildered and bamboozled, ought at least be able to grasp one key insight of economic thought, which worked out a theory of self-organizing complex systems long before this type of explanation became part of the standard repertoire of the physical and biological sciences during the second half of the twentieth century: self-organizing complex systems are capable of producing what are called emergent phenomena. These phenomena give the impression of being intentional, but in fact they are *subjectless* processes. It is altogether remarkable that the same expression, "subjectless processes," should have been used by both the champion of economic neoliberalism, Friedrich Hayek, and the father of structural Marxism, Louis Althusser. At the outset I likened "the markets" to a sluggish, craven, and dumb beast. But they might also be pictured as a gelatinous and porous blob (*The Blob* was a famous horror film, as it happens), dumb as well, but extremely dangerous, always lying in wait, ready to swallow up individuals and whole peoples—without, however, having the least ill *intention* toward any of them.

One can scarcely make war on a nonsubject, any more than one can restrain one's own fantasies through "regulation" of one sort or another. One treats them instead as one would an illness or disease, by trying to determine the cause. One doesn't issue absurd commands and ultimatums ("Listen here, my little neurotic obsession: from now on you are forbidden to take up more than 17% of my waking life"). The risibly belligerent determination of politicians to subject Economy to a regime of maximum ratios and limits is no more than the fig leaf and codpiece of political impotence. No, fatalism is definitely not to be found where everyone thinks to look for it.

Time, Paradox

And if it must needs be said that foreknowledge of events is not the cause of the occurrence of those events; for a foreknown sinner, when he sins, does not thereby hold God within his power—why, what is even more wonderful, we do in fact say that the event about to take place is the cause of the existence of the foreknowledge concerning it. For not because it is known does it take place; but because it is about to take place, it is known.

—Eusebius of Caesarea, *Preparation for the Gospel*, 6.11

One, therefore, may concede—provided we had the power of gaining so thorough an insight into a man's way of thinking, as it manifests itself in his actions, internal as well as external, that every motive force prompting him, even the least significant, became known to us, and that all external occasions having an effect upon these became known to us at the same time—that we could calculate the man's future conduct with the same degree of certitude as we can calculate the eclipse of the moon or the sun. Yet we should still be entitled to assert that man was a being endowed with freedom.

—Immanuel Kant, *Critique of Practical Reason*, 1.1.3

I n what follows I discuss a number of variations on Newcomb's paradox. Harmless to all appearances, it nonetheless constitutes a metaphysical bomb whose shock wave continues to overturn ideas long accepted to be true in fields as varied as rational theology, strategic thinking, social and political philosophy, ethics, economic theory, game theory, and the philosophy of rational choice.

Newcomb's paradox arises from the behavior of free agents in a deterministic universe. Conceived in the theoretical context of quantum physics, it challenges our intuitions about the nature of prediction, freedom, and determinism in a way that has seldom been equaled. Above all, it forces us to think deeply about the most difficult problem there is, the problem of time. Here I give a capsule summary of my own experience in trying to meet this challenge, which has shaped the course of my philosophical investigations ever since I first encountered it in connection with my early research in the philosophy of rational choice. I shall therefore begin with this topic.

Logic and Society

The strategic dominance principle was raised to the status of an axiomatic truth by one of the founders of modern decision theory, Leonard Savage. The logical form of this axiom, which Savage called the sure-thing principle (STP), is expressed in terms of preferences: if a subject prefers an option p to another option q in the case where the state of the world belongs to a subset E, and if he also prefers p to q in the complement of E, then rationality demands that he prefer p to q even if he does not know whether the state of the world belongs to E or to the complement of E.

The trouble with this logic is that it is responsible for a great many of the evils besetting modern societies. I am interested here in two things, first, the very great difficulty that people have in trusting one another, and second, their fundamental inability to manage disagreements in a way that does not harm everyone involved. If human beings are nevertheless able to live together in society, it is only by freeing themselves from the yoke of the logic formalized by Savage's principle. The question therefore arises, are social relations irrational?

Newcomb's paradox emerges from a situation in which common sense appears to conflict with STP. Let us review the terms of the paradox, as I described it in chapter 4.

Newcomb's Paradox

An agent is presented with two boxes. One of them is transparent, and visibly contains a thousand dollars; the other is opaque, and, he is told, may contain either a million dollars or nothing at all. The agent is given a choice between two strategies:

s1. Taking what is in the opaque box alone
s2. Taking what is in both boxes

At the moment when the choice is explained to the agent, a being who has the power to predict the agent's choices will already have placed a million dollars in the opaque box *if and only if* he has predicted that the agent will choose s1. The agent knows all this, and, what is more, has complete confidence in the predictive abilities of the predictor. What should he do?

One's first reaction is to say that the agent should choose s1. The predictor will have predicted this choice, and so the agent will have a million dollars. If he were to choose s2 he would have only a thousand dollars. The paradox is connected with the fact that another way of looking at the matter seems equally persuasive, although it leads to the opposite conclusion. When the agent makes his choice, either there are or there are not a million dollars in the opaque box: in taking what is in both boxes, he stands to win a thousand dollars more in either case than if he were to take only what is in the opaque box. S2 is therefore the dominant strategy.

Three out of four experimental subjects choose s1, in violation of STP. They each receive one million dollars. Professional philosophers are different from ordinary people: almost all of them choose s2 on the ground that it is the dominant strategy. As a result, each of them receives one thousand dollars—and, as a sort of consolation prize, the unshakable conviction that they are correct.

Should One Be a Compatibilist or Not?

Almost everyone who has spent hours, months, or even years racking his brain over Newcomb's paradox manages to convince himself at some point that he has found *the* solution. I myself am no exception to the rule—the difference being, of course, that my solution is the right one! Or at least, like everyone else, I believe mine is right. I owe my solution in part to the arguments of the analytic philosopher and Calvinist theologian Alvin Plantinga. Plantinga recognized in Newcomb's problem a terrible challenge to the traditional defense of compatibilism, which is to say the view that that there is no contradiction in asserting the existence both of an omniscient God and of persons endowed with free will, in the sense that they might act otherwise than they do.

William of Ockham's Solution

If God plays the role of Newcomb's predictor, his prescience is by definition *essential*, which is to say that it obtains in all possible worlds. Yet if the following incompatibilist argument is accepted, the existence of an essentially prescient God in this sense rules out the possibility of free will.

If God existed at time t_1 and predicted at t_1 that agent S would do X at a later time t_2, God's essential prescience is expressed by the following relation between two events:

(1) God existed at t_1 and predicted at t_1 that agent S would do X at t_2" *strictly implies* "S does X at t_2,

where strict implication is material implication¹ in all possible worlds. Given these same two premises, we also have:

(2) There is nothing that S can do at t_2 such that, if he were to do it, God would not have predicted at t_1 that S would do X at t_2.

This follows by virtue of the *principle of the fixity of the past*: the past is counterfactually independent of any present action. From (1) and (2) one derives:

(3) When an agent acts, if there exists an essentially prescient predictor at a moment prior to the action who predicts his action, the agent cannot act otherwise than he does.

Free will, in other words, is incompatible with essential prescience.

A classic way of avoiding this conclusion was devised in the fourteenth century by the English Franciscan monk William of Ockham, who denied that the principle of the fixity of the past applies to facts that do not *strictly* belong to the past. A prediction that God made at some past time cannot be considered to strictly belong to the past, if only because it strictly implies the truth of a proposition (traditionally known as a future contingent proposition, having the form "This free agent will do such-and-such a thing") that concerns a fact strictly belonging to the future. Where one is dealing with a *future contingent* proposition, in other words, since (2) no longer holds, (3) no longer follows.

The Challenge of Newcomb's Paradox and Plantinga's Solution

If God does not limit himself to predicting the future, but instead, as a *providential* God, intervenes in the world as a consequence of prediction—if, for example, he decides to place (or not place) a million dollars in a box, depending on whether (or not) he predicts that a free agent will choose to do such and such a thing—Ockham's solution is deprived of all its force. It is to Alvin Plantinga's great credit that he immediately grasped this on first encountering Newcomb's paradox.[2] The prediction that God made in the past may not be strictly about the past, but his action surely does strictly belong to the past.

Plantinga begins by showing that if God is assumed to be prescient *in all possible worlds*, (2) cannot properly be asserted. To say that at time t_2 S does X, as God predicted at t_1, presents no problem; but if the agent is supposed to be endowed with free will, the following counterfactual proposition must be held to be true, in contradiction of (2):

(4) If S were to do at t_2 something other than X, let us say Y, God would not have predicted at t_1 that S would do X at t_2, since God would have foreseen that he would do Y.

In other words, if the principle of the fixity of the past does not obtain, it is not because what God did in the past only apparently concerns the past (this might perhaps be said of his foresight, though certainly not of his action), but because the assumption of free will in the presence of an essentially prescient predictor implies that the agent is endowed with a *counterfactual power over the past*.

In Newcomb's problem, if we posit that the predictor is prescient in all possible worlds, this power is expressed thus:

(5) If the agent who chooses only what is in the opaque box (S1)—and, as a result, finds a million dollars in it—had chosen both boxes, he would have found the opaque box empty and would have had to content himself with the thousand dollars in the second box.

Rational choice theorists, who stubbornly cling to STP, dismiss the intuitive confidence of anyone who chooses to take what is in the opaque box alone on the ground that they grant themselves an inconceivable *causal* power over the past. What Plantinga's argument shows is that there is no need to posit the existence of such a power: a *counterfactual* power suffices to justify S1. This counterfactual power is the logical consequence of compatibilism.[3]

Projected Time

The Challenge of the Backward Induction Paradox

After mulling over Plantinga's solution for some time, I reluctantly had to admit that it was no more successful than the ones proposed by others before him. I was led to this conclusion by another paradox of rational choice theory, the backward induction paradox, which says that there exist situations in which the *counterfactual* power an agent possesses over the past *causally* prohibits him from acting in a certain way. Rescuing compatibilism from this difficulty plainly requires a much deeper metaphysics than the one developed by Plantinga.[4]

Consider, for example, what game theorists call an assurance game. Informally analyzed by Hobbes, Hume, and Kant, it may be described more formally with reference to a simple diagram (figure 3).

Figure 3. Assurance Game

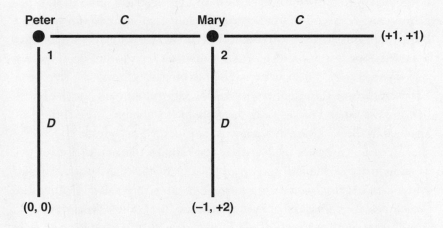

1, 2: times
C: cooperation; *D*: defection

In principle, a mutually advantageous exchange between Peter and Mary is possible that will lead them from their present state—vector (0, 0), the first element of which represents Peter's utility (or some other index supposed to order preferences), and the second Mary's utility—to a state (+1, +1), which each of them prefers. But if, for one reason or another, the exchange depends on Peter making the first move at time 1 (*C*), there is a risk that Mary will fail to cooperate, keeping what Peter gives her without giving him anything in return. In that case, by defecting (*D*) at time 2, Mary would wind up with +2, leaving Peter with −1.

Backward induction convinces us that the exchange cannot take place, even though it would improve the situation of each party. Let us look first at the last step, that is, at time 2, when it is Mary's turn to decide whether to cooperate or to defect. It is rational for her to defect since she obtains +2, as against +1 if she cooperates. Peter, on the other hand, at time 1, has a choice between making the first move (in which case he anticipates that Mary will not reciprocate and that he will end up with −1), and making no move, which is to say *D* (in which case his situation is unchanged, since he still has 0). Therefore he makes no move, and the exchange does not take place.

One is tempted to say that this mutually disadvantageous outcome could be avoided by resort to the institution of promising. Mary, since she stands to gain as much from cooperating as Peter, should promise him at time 0, before the game begins, that she will cooperate at 2 if he will cooperate at 1. But this is a futile hope! Mary knows perfectly well that when the time comes, which is to say time 2, she will be better off not keeping her promise. Peter, reading her mind, knows this too. Even if Mary swears to him on a stack of Bibles, her promise is not *credible.* Peter therefore makes no move. This is the form assumed by the backward induction paradox in the present case.[5]

I mentioned earlier, in chapter 4, that rational choice theorists (as well as enlightened capitalists) try to wriggle out of this difficulty by making ethics into a sort of deus ex machina. Sometimes they call it "confidence," sometimes "trust"—a kind of magic wand that brings about what rationality alone is powerless to achieve. Thus it is imagined that Mary, by breaking her promise to do what rationality tells her to do, will suffer pangs of conscience. But this amounts to divorcing ethics from rationality, right from the start. There must be a better way forward.

The idea occurred to me of treating the assurance game as though it were a variant of Newcomb's problem, with Peter taking the role of the essentially prescient predictor and Mary that of the agent. There are two important differences between the assurance game, reinterpreted in this way, and New-comb's problem in its original form. Like Newcomb's predictor, Peter reacts to his anticipation of Mary's choice, but he does so in a way that does not have the same appearance of arbitrariness since he maximizes his payoff by regarding Mary's action as fixed. That is the first difference. To understand the second, let us reason as Mary does at the outset of the game in trying to make up her mind what to do in the event it is her turn to decide at time 2:

(6) If it were my turn to decide at 2 and I were to choose C, Peter would have foreseen this at 1 and, seeking to maximize his own payoff, would himself have chosen C, leaving the next move to me. We would then each have +1.

(7) If it were my turn to decide at 2 and I were to choose D, Peter would have foreseen this at 1 and, seeking to maximize his own payoff, would himself have chosen D, which means that it would not have been my turn to choose at 2.

Since the two premises of (7) lead to a contradiction, each one entails the negation of the other. Accordingly:

(8) If it were Mary's turn to choose at 2, she would choose *C*.

Peter at 1 is capable of simulating Mary's reasoning. If he chooses *C*, given (8) and (6), he ends up with +1, as against the 0 that would be his if he were to choose *D*. He therefore cooperates, as does Mary, and the mutually advantageous trade takes place—thus reconciling rationality and ethics.

And yet Mary's counterfactual power over the past, manifested by the disjunction between (6) and (7), appears to vanish into thin air, along with her free will, since it is impossible for her to choose *D*. What exactly is the nature of this impossibility? Can the compatibility of free will and essential prescience still be salvaged?

The way out I have proposed is this. *Before* Mary acts, she is free to choose between *C* and *D*. If choosing *D* is possible, this is because, insofar as Mary has not yet acted, the past—in the event, Peter's choice—is still indeterminate (the German term used in quantum theory is "*unbestimmt*"). It is only when Mary makes up her mind to act that her past is determined. If she were to choose *D*, she would be prevented from acting. It seems as though she would never have been able to choose *D*, but *this impossibility only exists in retrospect.*

The metaphysical price to be paid for salvaging free will is that we must dispense not only with the principle of the fixity of the past, but also with the principle of *the reality* of the past. It is here that the true significance of Newcomb's paradox can be seen: it succeeds in reproducing on the macroscopic scale of human behavior a philosophical enigma that concerns the world of quantum information.

Once Mary has acted, it appears that she could never have acted otherwise, and yet before she acted it was possible for her to act otherwise. The future, in other words, is necessary, but not until it occurs; once realized, it appears to be fixed, which is to say counterfactually independent of present action. This combination of the past's indeterminacy, so long as an agent has not acted, and the fixity of the future, once an action has taken place, defines a quite particular metaphysics of temporality that I call *projected time.*

Action in this metaphysics suddenly bursts forth, as though from nothingness, and creates a state of retrospective necessity in the same way that, in the philosophy of Bergson (and his student Sartre), an event becomes possible only in making itself possible. More formally, we may say that the truth value of propositions containing modal elements of possibility and necessity are indexed to the moment when such propositions are uttered.

The Metaphysics of Projected Time

The metaphysics of projected time assumes the form of a loop in which past and future are mutually determining (figure 4).

To predict the future in projected time amounts to seeking the fixed point of a loop that unites an anticipation (from the past about the future) and a causally produced event (of the future, produced by the past). The predictor, knowing that his prediction is going to have causal effects in the world, is bound to take them into account if he wishes the future to conform to what he has predicted. Traditionally, which is to say in a world dominated by religion (as we saw earlier in chapter 2), this figure was the prophet—most especially, the biblical prophet. Here, however, I am speaking of prophecy in a purely secular and technical sense. A prophet is someone who seeks the *fixed point* of a problem, which is to say the point at which freely willed action achieves the very thing that fate ordains. A prophecy sees itself as bringing about what it announces as destiny.

Prophets in this sense are legion in modern democratic societies wedded to science and technology. Personal experience of projected time is institutionally sponsored and organized; indeed, in much of daily life it simply cannot be avoided. Voices of greater or lesser authority are constantly telling us what the more or less near future will bring: tomorrow's highway traffic, the result of next month's elections, the rates of inflation and growth during the coming year, the change in greenhouse-gas emissions over the next decade, and so on. These prophets, whom we call *forecasters*, know perfectly well—no less well than we do ourselves—that we are the ones who make this future, which they announce as though it had been decided in advance and for all eternity. And yet we do not protest against something that might be considered scandalous from the metaphysical point of view, unless occasionally—when we go to the polls to vote, for example. What I have tried to bring

Figure 4. Projected Time

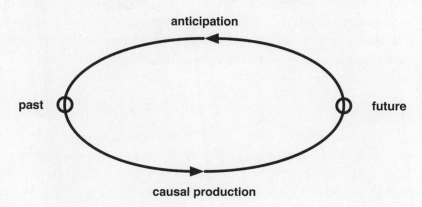

anticipation

past   future

causal production

out here is the logical consistency of this way of coordinating behavior by means of the future.

In the second chapter, I mentioned Pierre Massé's memorable characterization of the aim of French postwar economic planning as "achieving by concerted deliberation and study an image of the future that is sufficiently optimistic to be desirable and sufficiently credible to give rise to actions that will bring about its own realization." This formula makes sense only within the metaphysics of projected time, whose loop linking past and future it perfectly describes. On that view, coordinated collective behavior springs from a shared *conception* of the future that is capable of closing the loop between the causal production of the future and its self-fulfilling expectation.

From Nuclear Deterrence to Enlightened Doomsaying

In the metaphysics of projected time, any event that is not situated on a universe line, defined as the sequence of all events that occur, is held to be impossible. In other words, all possible events occur. It follows from this that prudence can never take the form of prevention. Prevention implies that the undesirable event one prevents from happening is an unactualized possibility. The event must be possible in order for us to have a reason to act; but if our action is effective, the event does not occur. This is unimaginable in projected time, in which all possibilities occur. What may appear at first sight to be not merely bizarre, but also a fatal weakness of the metaphysics of projected time, is in fact a source of great strength in helping us to think intelligently about the gravest threats that presently weigh upon the future of humanity.

The Logic of MAD

Consider the following game, which formalizes the situation known as mutually assured destruction (MAD). Alter contemplates attacking Ego. If Alter actually does attack, Ego has a choice between yielding—in which case he loses, for example, some part of his territory or zone of influence—and counterattacking—in which case the escalation of violence spells disaster for both belligerents (figure 5).

This diagram illustrates a zero-sum game played on the edge of the abyss. Backward induction leads us to conclude that the deterrent threat "If you, Alter, attack me, I, Ego, will launch a counterattack that will annihilate both of us" is not credible.[6] Finding himself at 2, Ego, after having been attacked by Alter, will find it prudent to do Y. Alter therefore attacks at 1 and Ego yields at 2. This problem, the noncredibility of the threat on which nuclear deterrence rests, makes up the better part of the strategic literature on the subject. What statesman, having in the aftermath of a first strike only remnants of a devastated nation left to defend, would run the risk, by launching a retaliatory strike out of a desire for vengeance, of putting an end to the human race?

Can an argument based on projected time salvage the effectiveness of deterrence? The argument from prevention with which I began gives cause for doubt. Could it be that the response R (known as escalation—Clausewitz's "tendency to the extreme") constitutes the fixed point of the loop between past and future that defines the metaphysics of projected time? Alter's anticipation at 1 of Ego's choice at 2 to do R would prevent Ego from deciding at 2, since Alter would then refrain from attacking. The loop is joined together at a fixed point only if Ego yields and Alter attacks. The conclusion is therefore the same as the one arrived at by backward induction: deterrence is ineffective. And yet the reason why deterrence is ineffective in projected time is no longer the noncredibility of the threat, but the self-refuting character of perfectly successful deterrence.

Figure 5. Mutually Assured Destruction

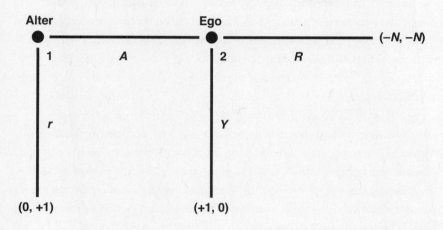

r: renounces   R: retaliates

A: attacks   Y: yields

N: very large number

Left-hand number: Alter's payoff

Right-hand number: Ego's payoff

The argument usually encountered in the technical literature on the subject assumes the following form. For a deterence regime—the criminal justice system, for example—to be effective, it is necessary that it not be 100% effective. It has to be understood that anyone who commits a crime runs a very high risk of going to jail: criminals are punished. But a single failure in the MAD case, signifying nuclear apocalypse, would be fatal. Nuclear deterrence, to be effective, *must* be totally effective. But if it is totally effective, it is not effective at all. Therefore deterrence is not effective. On closer examination, however, it becomes plain that this argument is valid only if one reasons in terms of projected time. To say that deterrence is effective is to say that Alter refrains because Ego does R at 2; and that if Ego were to do R at 2, Ego would not have had any decision to make at 2. A counterattack by Ego is therefore not part of the universe line. Escalation R being impossible, the deterrent threat disappears and Alter has no reason not to attack.

Since the MAD regime protected the world from nuclear catastrophe for more than forty years during the Cold War, or so it would appear, the problem remains of explaining how this miracle could have occurred. Strategists belatedly took a decisive step toward such an explanation when they realized that deterrence ought to function without any deterrent *intention.* In principle, the mere *existence* of two deadly arsenals pointed at each other, without the least threat of their use being made or even implied, is enough to keep the warheads locked away in their silos. Even so, the specter of nuclear apocalypse did not disappear from the picture. Under the name *existential deterrence*, the perils of the old game were transformed in such a way that mutual annihilation now loomed as the *fate* of humanity, its destiny. To say that deterrence worked means simply this: so long as one does not recklessly tempt fate, there is a chance that it will forget about us—for a time, perhaps a long, indeed a very long time; but not forever.

Let us come back to the formalism of projected time. There does in fact exist another fixed point than the one that makes deterrence ineffective, if one makes allowance for an *imperfection* in the closing of the loop—an imperfection that is inscribed in the future as our fate. The resulting uncertainty is what makes deterrence effective. But the uncertainty in this case is not a matter of probability. Let us assign it a weight equal to epsilon, ε, by definition small or very small. Existential deterrence may then be succinctly characterized: because there is a weight ε that deterrence will not work, the weight attached to its working is $1 - \varepsilon$. What might seem at first to be a tautology (as it obviously is in the metaphysics of occurring time, where weights represent probabilities) cannot be one here, since the preceding proposition is not true for $\varepsilon = 0$.[7] The condition that the weight attached to deterrence's not working have a strictly positive value is what inscribes catastrophe in the future; and it is because catastrophe is inscribed in the future that deterrence is effective—*barring an accident of weight* ε. Note, by the way, that it would be altogether incorrect to say that it is the *possibility* of error, having a probability ε, that guarantees the effectiveness of deterrence—as if error and the absence of error constituted the two branches of a bifurcation. There is no forking path in projected time. The error is not only possible, it is actual—written down by a slip of the pen, as it were.

Enlightened Doomsaying

What makes it legitimate to liken the threat posed to the survival of humanity by major catastrophes (especially the disruption of the earth's climate and ecosystems) to nuclear deterrence is precisely the interpretation of deterrence in existential terms. The logical structure in both cases is the same: not a fight to the death between two adversaries, but a sole protagonist, mankind, forced to confront the reified and externalized effects of its own violence. What is more, the obstacle to stimulating awareness and action is identical: even when one knows what is going to happen, the catastrophe is not credible. We know, or we ought to know, but we do not believe what we know.

Enlightened doomsaying is a ruse that consists in acting as though we were the victims of fate while keeping in mind that we are the sole cause of our misfortune. From now on we must live with our eyes trained on this unthinkable event, the self-destruction of humanity, with the objective, not of making it impossible, which would be a contradiction, but of postponing the moment of truth as long as possible. This requires that individual behaviors be coordinated with reference to a negative purpose, namely, of avoiding a fixed future *that we do not wish for ourselves.* And yet the paradox of self-refutation lingers: if we succeed in avoiding an undesirable future, how can we be said to have acted in unison with our eyes trained on the future if the future has no existence? Enlightened doomsaying must therefore be formulated by recasting the formula of French planning I mentioned earlier in negative terms, only qualifying it in one crucial respect in order to escape self-contradiction. This yields the following maxim: To devise, by means of scientific modeling and philosophical inquiry into the aims and purposes of mankind, an image of the future that is sufficiently catastrophic to be repellent and sufficiently credible to produce behavior that will prevent it from being realized, *barring an accident.*

In the words of the poet, "Yet where danger lurks, grows also that which saves."[8]

Notes

Introduction. The Bewilderment of Politics

1. In the French edition, I called this giant figure a "cold monster"—thinking of Nietzsche's famous phrase in *Thus Spoke Zarathustra,* "State is the name of the coldest of cold monsters." Nietzsche goes on to say that it coldly tells lies as well, and never more coldly than when it says, "I, the state, am the people." Hobbes's frontispiece beautifully anticipated this idea: the giant's body encompasses the people, but it has a head, which is distinct from the people and which dominates it.

2. Note that the biblical text employs a singular verb whose subject is nevertheless morphologically plural, in the same way that today one says, for example, "The United States is a great country." Thus in the article "Genesis," added to the third edition (1765) of Voltaire's *Dictionnaire philosophique,* one reads: "'In the beginning God created [*Dieu créa*] the heavens and the earth.' That is how it is translated, but the translation is inaccurate. There is no moderately educated man who does not know that the text says: 'In the beginning the gods made [*firent*, pl.] or the gods made [*fit*, sing.] the heavens and the earth.'"

3. *Forbidden Planet* (1956), based on a screenplay by Cyril Hume and starring Walter Pidgeon and Anne Francis.

4. From an article posted at www.lemonde.fr (16 November 2011).

5. Here is another example, selected almost at random and likewise posted at www.lemonde.fr (21 November 2011), following the legislative elections in Spain: "Greece, Ireland, Portugal, Italy, Spain: all these countries have been shaken by the markets, which *did not hesitate*, in the Spanish case, to tighten the screws on the eve of the elections" (my emphasis). The market—the one God, referred to here by its plural form—*knows* what it wants and what it is doing; it has a plan, it deliberates, and sometimes moves with great speed when a favorable opportunity presents itself. How can one fail to be indignant, faced with an utter lack of indignation on the part of all those

who are witnesses to this shocking abuse of language—in speaking of the market as though it were a person capable of forming intentions and carrying out plans—and who yet remain silent?

6. "Encore un instant, Monsieur le bourreau!" Proverbial in French, though probably apocryphal as well, these are said to have been the last words uttered by Madame du Barry, Louis XV's last official mistress, on climbing the stairs to the guillotine in December 1793.—Trans.

7. The economists Christopher Sims and Thomas Sargent, quoted by www.lemonde.fr (10 October 2011). The emphasis in the first instance is mine.

8. The French word *l'économie* refers to each of two things that are distinguished in English, the economy and economics. The original title of my book, *L'avenir de l'économie,* therefore carries a double meaning that is signified by "Economy," the neologism I have introduced at the head of this paragraph.

9. See Milton Friedman and Rose D. Friedman, *Free to Choose: A Personal Statement* (New York: Harcourt Brace Jovanovich, 1980).

10. A personal aside: my criticism in this book—very harsh criticism, as I am the first to recognize—is directed at the economics *profession*, and not by any means at every one of its members. Many of them are remarkable for their intelligence and their discernment, and I am proud to be able to count a good number of these ones among my friends. But if they are remarkable, it is in spite of their belonging to this professional milieu, and not because of it. I myself taught economics at the École Polytechnique in Paris for a dozen years before devoting myself to philosophy. I do not regret this apprenticeship in the least, for what it taught me is indispensable for anyone who aspires to do important work in social, moral, and political philosophy—only in this case not in spite of the discipline's failures, but rather because of them. The profession itself, however, is another matter. Its organizational structure, its mode of recruitment, the false prestige it enjoys from an international prize, the Nobel, that it does not deserve, the excessive regard for mathematical dexterity—all these things have made it a conservative discipline, in the worst sense of this term, and among all the disciplines that make up what is now a truly global system of research and higher education perhaps the one least capable of reforming itself.

11. Alexis de Tocqueville, *Democracy in America*, trans. Gerald E. Bevan (London: Penguin, 2003), 2.2.13, 626. [Bevan rather too loosely translates both *bien-être* and *bien-être matériel* as "prosperity," hence the modifications to his version made here.—Trans.]

Chapter 1. Economy and the Problem of Evil

1. This view is brilliantly argued by Susan Neiman in *Evil in Modern Thought: An Alternative History of Philosophy,* 2nd ed. (Princeton, N.J.: Princeton University Press, 2004).

2. See Alain Renaut, *The Era of the Individual: A Contribution to a History of Subjectivity*, trans. M. B. DeBevoise and Franklin Phillip (Princeton, N.J.: Princeton University Press, 1997), 79–83.

3. Jean-Jacques Rousseau, *Émile: or, On Education* (1762), book 4, trans. Allan Bloom (New York: Basic Books, 1979), 282.

4. See Jean-Pierre Dupuy, "Invidious Sympathy in *The Theory of Moral Sentiments,*" *Adam Smith Review* 2 (2006): 96–121.

5. Jean-Jacques Rousseau, *Rousseau, Judge of Jean-Jacques: Dialogues*, in *The Collected Writings of Rousseau*, ed. and trans. Roger D. Masters and Christopher Kelly, 13 vols. (Hanover, N.H.: University Press of New England, 1990–2009), 1:9. The emphasis is mine. Here and elsewhere I

have modified the English translations found in this edition, which not infrequently suffer from grave errors of interpretation.

6. See Jean-Jacques Rousseau, *Letter to Beaumont* (1763), in Masters and Kelly, *Collected Writings of Rousseau*, 9:28–29.

7. Günther Anders, "L'homme sur le pont: Journal d'Hiroshima et de Nagasaki," in *Hiroshima est partout*, trans. Ariel Morabia with the assistance of Françoise Cazenave, Denis Trierweiler, and Gabriel Raphaël Veyret (Paris: Seuil, 2008), 168. The emphasis is mine. I have deliberately modified the French translation with reference to the implicit meaning of the original German text.

8. Hannah Arendt, *Eichmann in Jerusalem: A Report on the Banality of Evil*, rev. and aug. ed. (New York: Viking, 1965), 287.

9. Quoted in ibid., 277.

10. Émile Durkheim, *The Elementary Forms of Religious Life*, ed. Mark S. Cladis and trans. Carol Cosman (New York: Oxford University Press, 2001), 313–14. The emphasis is mine. [Cosman's version slightly modified.—Trans.]

11. Ibid., 314 n. 1.

12. Voltaire, *Poem on the Lisbon Disaster*, in appendix 2 of *Candide, or Optimism*, ed. and trans. Theo Cuffe (New York: Penguin, 2005), 106. [The last line in Cuffe's version contains the plural "misfortunes," evidently a misprint.—Trans.]

13. Ibid.

14. See Adam Smith, *The Theory of Moral Sentiments*, ed. Ryan Patrick Hanley (New York: Penguin, 2009), 1.3.3, 73.

15. See John Maynard Keynes, *The General Theory of Employment, Interest, and Money*, 6.22 (London: Macmillan, 1936), 313–32; also my discussion below in chapter 2 ("Two Avatars of Torture").

16. Albert O. Hirschman, *The Passions and the Interests: Political Arguments for Capitalism before Its Triumph* (Princeton, N.J.: Princeton University Press, 1977), 132. Italics in the original, removed here.

17. Friedrich A. Hayek, *Individualism and Economic Order* (London: Routledge & Kegan Paul, 1949), 24.

18. I have done this elsewhere. See the chapter on Hayek in my book *Le sacrifice et l'envie* (Paris: Calmann-Lévy, 1992), 241–91.

19. See Friedrich A. Hayek, *The Road to Serfdom* (Chicago: University of Chicago Press, 1944), 106.

20. At the suggestion of the Viennese psychiatrist and Auschwitz survivor Viktor Frankl, whose unforgettable book *Man's Quest for Meaning* (1946) had greater influence in English-speaking countries during the 1950s than Freud's own work.

21. See the chapter on Adam Smith and invidious sympathy in *Le sacrifice et l'envie*, 75–106.

22. Élie Halévy did much to popularize this view in the last century; see *The Growth of Philosophic Radicalism*, trans. Mary Morris (New York: Macmillan, 1928), 1.3.1, 97–107.

23. This, alas, is Hirschman's own interpretation; see *The Passions and the Interests*, 2.2, 100–113. The doctrine of natural harmony is famously stated with reference to an "invisible hand" in the second chapter of the fourth book of *The Wealth of Nations*.

24. See René Girard, *Violence and the Sacred*, trans. Patrick Gregory (Baltimore: Johns Hopkins University Press, 1977), especially 256–60.

25. See Paul Dumouchel and Jean-Pierre Dupuy, *L'enfer des choses: René Girard et la logique de l'économie* (Paris: Seuil, 1979).

26. The Hegelian tradition speaks instead of self-exteriorization (*Entäusserung*).

27. Thus the subtitle of Mandeville's *Fable of the Bees* (1714).

28. Johann Wolfgang Goethe, *Faust, A Tragedy*, Part One, scene 6, Faust's Study (i),11.1335–36, trans. David Luke (New York: Oxford University Press, 1987), 42.

29. In the phrase of Adam Ferguson, another figure of the Scottish Enlightenment often quoted by Hayek, social order is "the result of human action, but not the execution of any human design." See Ferguson, *An Essay on the History of Civil Society* (1767), 3.2 (Edinburgh: Edinburgh University Press, 1966), 122.

30. See especially Smith, *Theory of Moral Sentiments*, 4.1, 212–13.

31. Friedman and Friedman, *Free to Choose*, 13. I have taken the liberty of reversing the order in which these sentences appear in the Friedmans' text, while adding emphasis.

32. Tocqueville, *Democracy in America*, 2.2.13, 624–25. Again, the emphasis is mine.

33. Anders, "L'homme sur le pont," in *Hiroshima est partout*, 171–72.

Chapter 2. Self-Transcendence

1. Or, according to another version, by his bootstraps. Rudolf Erich Raspe published *The Surprising Adventures of Baron Münchausen* in London in 1785. The tales were translated back into German, and new ones added in a definitive edition that appeared in Göttingen the following year. Since then, owing to some perplexing detours through quantum mechanics and the emigration of German scientists to the United States before World War II, the related notion of "bootstrapping" has come to be a part of the English language. Thus, for example, to use a common expression borrowed from computer science, one "boots up" a computer by starting its operating system: a simple program activates another, more complex program.

2. Friedrich Nietzsche, *On the Genealogy of Morals*, 2.1, trans. Walter Kaufmann and R. J. Hollingdale (New York: Random House, 1967), 58. [Here the Kaufmann/Hollingdale translation has been preferred to newer versions by Diethe (Cambridge, 1994) and Smith (Oxford, 1996).—Trans.]

3. Maurice Godelier famously developed this argument in the 1960s: "Neoclassical theory typically assumes that the firm is unable to modify market prices, but can only adapt itself to them; and yet this *contradicts* the general assumption that each economic agent contributes to the formation of prices through the goods he supplies and demands." See *Rationalité et irrationalité en économie* (Paris: Maspero, 1966), 33; the emphasis is mine.

4. See, for example, Niall Ferguson, *Virtual History: Alternatives and Counterfactuals* (London: Picador, 1997).

5. Further to my discussion of this concept in chapter 1, I use the term "specularity" to refer to a particular cognitive activity in which one person simulates the thought of another by taking into account the fact that the other person does the same thing with regard to him, creating an endless and bottomless *mise en abyme* in the same fashion that the reflections cast by two facing mirrors

inside an armoire are repeated indefinitely. The same image occurred to Adam Smith's friend David Hume, that other commanding figure of the Scottish Enlightenment: "The minds of men are mirrors to one another." See Hume, *A Treatise of Human Nature*, ed. David Fate Norton and Mary J. Norton, 2.2.5 (Oxford: Oxford University Press, 2000), 236.

6. An important branch of economic thought, known as the economics of conventions, has applied this concept over the past twenty-five years in various fields of research, from monetary policy to labor relations. Founded by a group of French economists, it took its inspiration from a work by the great metaphysician David K. Lewis, *Convention: A Philosophical Study* (Cambridge, Mass.: Harvard University Press, 1969).

7. This choice was probably due to the decisive influence of the French economist Léon Walras, an expatriate teaching in Lausanne, on the early development of the so-called theory of general equilibrium. Trained as an engineer at the École des Mines in Paris, Walras had been influenced in his turn by the mathematician Augustin Cournot, a friend and mentor of his father, the economist Auguste Walras. Cournot, an authority on rational mechanics, is remembered still today for his work in economic theory, particularly in connection with market competition.

8. The philosopher John Searle, in his devastating critique of the strong form of artificial intelligence, has particularly insisted on this point. To recall his favorite example, a computer simulation of the biochemical processes involved in eating a pizza is not at all the same thing as the actual digestion of the pizza itself. See "Minds, Brains, and Computers," *Behavioural and Brain Sciences* 3 (1980): 417–57.

9. David K. Lewis, "Counterfactual Dependence and Time's Arrow" (1979), reprinted with postscripts in *Philosophical Papers*, vol. 2 (Oxford: Oxford University Press, 1986), 38. The emphasis is mine.

10. Hans Jonas, *The Imperative of Responsibility: In Search of an Ethics for the Technological Age* (Chicago: University of Chicago Press, 1984), 113–14. The emphasis in the last sentence is mine.

11. The expression itself is usually credited to the sociologist Robert K. Merton. See "The Self-Fulfilling Prophecy," *Antioch Review* 8 (Summer 1948): 193–210.

12. Thus, for example, one reads in an editorial in *Le Monde* (6 September 2011): "One understands the reluctance of our leaders to sound the alarm. The head of the World Bank, the American Robert Zoellick, a wise man, insisted [today] that there is no threat of recession in the United States. Dilemma: to speak of *the situation as it really is*, one risks making economic agents still more discouraged, thereby *causing a prophecy of doom to come true*." Thus, too, Jacques Delors—an honest man if ever there was one, and no less wise than Zoellick: "I said three weeks ago that the euro was on the brink of the abyss. People said that this would only frighten the markets, but alas *events have proved me right*." Quoted in ibid.; my emphasis in both cases.

13. As the economic journalist Alain Faujas pointed out, commenting on the Group of Seven meeting held in Marseille on 9–10 September 2011, there is "an enormous discrepancy between the demand for economic leadership on the part of public opinion and the caution of the G7 heads of state, *who fear triggering an upheaval either by their public declarations or by their silence*. Perhaps the G7 should revert to its original practice of holding unannounced meetings, with no journalists present? 'Someone in the press would learn of the meeting,' observed one member, 'and that would be even worse, for its secrecy would be seen as proof of the seriousness of the situation.' . . . Mission Impossible for the G7." *Le Monde* (13 September 2011); my emphasis.

14. Or *"futuribles,"* a phrase popularized by the philosopher and political economist Bertrand de Jouvenel, who created the technique of futurism with Gaston Berger in the early 1960s. See Jouvenel, *The Art of Conjecture*, trans. Nikita Lary (New York: Basic Books, 1967).

15. A felicitous phrase due to the eminent futurist Jacques Lesourne in *Les mille sentiers de l'avenir* (Paris: Seghers, 1981).

16. A proposition is said to be common knowledge in a given population if it is true, if each person knows that it is true, if each person knows that each person knows that it is true, and so on indefinitely. The precise sense of this final clause is highly problematic. See Jean-Pierre Dupuy, "Common Knowledge, Common Sense," *Theory and Decision* 27 (1989): 37–62.

17. See André Orléan, "L'autoréférence dans la théorie keynésienne de la spéculation," *Cahiers d'Économie Politique* 14–15 (1988): 229–242.

18. Consider just these few recent examples of expert opinion. Alan Greenspan, then the chairman of the Federal Reserve: "[A] national severe price distortion [in housing] seems most unlikely in the United States" (19 October 2004); Dominique Strauss-Kahn, just after being appointed managing director of the International Monetary Fund: "The subprime crisis will have no dramatic effects on growth" (1 October 2007); his successor, Christine Lagarde, then finance and economy minister in France: "The real estate crisis and the financial crisis do not appear to have had any real effect on the American real economy. There is no reason to think that [they] will have an effect on the French real economy" (5 November 2007). These and other leading figures are quoted in the excellent short book on the crisis by Christian Walter and Michel de Pracontal, *Le virus B: Crise financière et mathématiques* (Paris: Seuil, 2009).

19. Deuteronomy 18:21–22. The emphasis is mine.

20. The road to regulatory hell is paved with good intentions. Regulators in America, and then elsewhere, reaffirmed their trust in the ability of rating agencies whose culpable blindness in the banking crisis of 2007–2008 was clear to properly evaluate the risk that a bank or a country would default on its obligations. When the sovereign debt of a country like Greece is downgraded, the predictable result is that institutional investors will withdraw en masse, some being legally obligated to do so. If the objective was to protect creditors against the risk of default by debtors, no better means of achieving the opposite result could have been devised. How are we to explain this fiasco? There is only one possibility: a willful ignorance of how self-transcendence works in financial markets.

21. This according to the most recent Intergovernmental Panel on Climate Change Assessment Report, published in 2007. A revised forecast, the fifth in an ongoing series of assessments, is expected to be completed in 2014.

22. The percentages in brackets indicate the proportions in which the respondents chose the corresponding option. In problem 1, for example, 78% of the subjects preferred option A, while the rest, 22%, preferred option B. Here I reproduce Tversky and Kahneman's exposition in "The Framing of Decisions and the Psychology of Choice," *Science* 211, no. 4481 (30 January 1981): 455.

23. See Maurice Allais, "Le comportement de l'homme rationnel devant le risque: Critique des postulats et axiomes de l'École américaine." *Econometrica* 21, no. 4 (1953): 503–46.

24. See Daniel Kahneman and Amos Tversky, "Prospect Theory: An Analysis of Decision under Risk," *Econometrica* 47, no. 2 (1979): 272.

25. See their essay "Conflict Resolution: A Cognitive Perspective," in *Barriers to Conflict Resolution*, ed. Kenneth J. Arrow et al. (New York: W. W. Norton, 1995), 53.

26. See Leda Cosmides and John Tooby, "Are Humans Good Intuitive Statisticians After All? Rethinking Some Conclusions from the Literature on Judgment under Uncertainty," *Cognition* 58 (1996): 1–73.

27. Éric Le Boucher, "Le protocole de Kyoto est moribond, achevons-le!" *Le Monde* (4 July 2004).

28. See Dumouchel and Dupuy, *L'enfer des choses*, 53–96; and Jean-Pierre Dupuy, *Libéralisme et justice sociale: Le sacrifice et l'envie* (Paris: Hachette, 1997), 11–45.

29. These expressions were coined and popularized by three of the leading figures of so-called second-order cybernetics, Heinz von Foerster, Henri Atlan, and Francisco Varela. On this tradition and its relationship to the original cybernetic movement, and to cognitive science in general, see Jean-Pierre Dupuy, *On the Origins of Cognitive Science: The Mechanization of the Mind*, trans. M. B. DeBevoise (Cambridge, Mass.: MIT Press, 2009), especially 10–11, 109–10, 119–23.

30. One hundred years before Darwin, Buffon speculated in his *Natural History* that humans and apes might share a common ancestor.

31. Named after the Hungarian-American mathematician George Pólya, who taught at ETH in Zurich (where his students included John von Neumann) before coming to Stanford in 1940.

32. See Jean-Pierre Dupuy, *La panique*, rev. and aug. ed. (Paris: Les Empêcheurs de Penser en Rond / Seuil, 2003), 57–78.

33. See Sigmund Freud, *Group Psychology and the Analysis of the Ego*, ed. and trans. James Strachey (New York: W. W. Norton, 1975), 29.

34. See Durkheim, *The Elementary Forms of Religious Life*, 2.7.2, 154–62.

35. Elias Canetti, *Crowds and Power*, trans. Carol Stewart (London: Gollancz, 1962), 29.

36. Recalled from memory, from a show aired on WNET (Channel 13 in New York), 29 October 2011; my emphasis.

37. The proposition that supply creates its own demand is known as Say's law (or law of markets), after the French economist and businessman Jean-Baptiste Say. It is remembered today mainly through Keynes's refutation of it in the first book of *The General Theory of Employment, Interest, and Money* (1936).

38. I summarize here the so-called theory of fixed-price equilibrium with rationing developed by French economists in the 1980s with the aim of strengthening the foundations of Keynesian theory; see, for example, Edmond Malinvaud, *The Theory of Unemployment Reconsidered*, 2nd ed. (New York: Blackwell, 1985). In retrospect it should be plain that what this theory lacks is a model of self-transcendence.

39. See the appendix concerning the theory of counterproductivity ("À la recherche du temps gagné") that I contributed to the second French edition of Illich's work on transportation, *Énergie et équité* (Paris: Seuil, 1975), 73–80; also Jean-Pierre Dupuy and Jean Robert, *La trahison de l'opulence* (Paris: Presses Universitaires de France, 1976).

40. See Hannah Arendt, *The Human Condition*, 2nd ed. (Chicago: University of Chicago Press, 1998), 243–47.

41. The etymological kinship between *finance*, a word that came into English from French and that originally meant "ransom," and the modern French word *fin*, or "end," derives from the Old French verb *finer*, meaning "to pay" or "to settle"—an alternate form of *finir* (to conclude, get through, extinguish).

42. Quoted in Roger Guesnerie, *L'économie de marché* (Paris: Flammarion, 1996), 75.

43. See Hobbes's introduction to *Leviathan: Or the Matter, Forme, & Power of a Common-Wealth*

Ecclesiasticall and Civill, ed. Ian Shapiro (New Haven: Yale University Press, 2010), 9; also 1.14.4, 80; 1.14.18, 84; and 2.17.13, 105.

44. Jean-Jacques Rousseau, Letter to Mirabeau (26 July 1767), in *The Social Contract and Other Later Political Writings*, ed. Victor Gourevitch (Cambridge: Cambridge University Press, 1997), 270. The same idea occurs later in *Considerations on the Government of Poland and on Its Planned Reformation* (1772): "To put law over man is a problem in politics which I compare to that of squaring the circle in geometry." See Masters and Kelly, *Collected Writings of Rousseau*, 11:170.

45. Rousseau, Letter to Mirabeau, in *The Social Contract*, 270; see also *Considerations on the Government of Poland*, §1, in Masters and Kelly, *Collected Writings of Rousseau*, 11:170.

46. Tocqueville, *Democracy in America*, 2.1.1, 493.

47. Ibid., 494. [Bevan's version slightly modified for the sake of clarity.—Trans.]

48. Ibid., 2.1.2, 500.

49. In my own work I have often called such points of reference "endogenous fixed points." See, for example, my concluding essay of this title in the Cerisy colloquium volume edited by Mark R. Anspach, *Jean-Pierre Dupuy: Dans l'œil du cyclone* (Paris: Carnets Nord, 2008), 297–316.

50. Tocqueville, *Democracy in America*, 2.1.2, 501.

51. Ibid.

52. See André Orléan's remarkable analysis of these ideas in *The Empire of Value: A New Foundation for Economics*, trans. M. B. DeBevoise (Cambridge, Mass.: MIT Press, 2014).

53. See Keynes's discussion of the "uncontrollable and disobedient psychology of the business world" in *The General Theory of Employment, Interest, and Money*, 6.22.2, 315–20.

54. Durkheim, *The Elementary Forms of Religious Life*, 2.7.2, 158.

55. Freud, in developing his theory of group psychology, failed to detect the operation of this mechanism. See my discussion in *La panique*, 57–78.

56. See the prologue to Jean-Pierre Dupuy, *The Mark of the Sacred*, trans. M. B. DeBevoise (Stanford, Calif.: Stanford University Press, 2013), 1–19.

Chapter 3. The Economics of the End and the End of Economics

1. See Carl von Clausewitz, *On War*, ed. and trans. Michael Howard and Peter Paret (Princeton, N.J.: Princeton University Press, 1976), 1.3.1, 76–77.

2. Murakami used this phrase in criticizing the use of nuclear energy in his speech accepting the Catalonia International Prize, 10 June 2011.

3. See Jean-Pierre Dupuy, *Petite métaphysique des tsunamis* (Paris: Seuil, 2005), 89–90.

4. The statistical estimates found in the literature vary markedly. One study on the Medicare system in the United States gives a figure of 30%; see Brigitte Dormont, "Les dépenses de santé: Une augmentation salutaire?," in *16 nouvelles questions d'économie contemporaine*, ed. Philippe Askenazy and Daniel Cohen (Paris: Pluriel, 2010), 395. A highly controversial article published by Dr. Luc Perino in the 1 July 2010 issue of *Le Monde*, "La mort et le PIB," gives a figure of 80% in the case of France.

5. Dormont, "Les dépenses de santé," 396.

6. See my book with Serge Karsenty, *L'invasion pharmaceutique*, 2nd ed. (Paris: Seuil, 1977).

7. Jean-Claude Beaune, "Le remède et sa guérison," in *La philosophie du remède*, ed. Jean-Claude Beaune (Seyssel: Champ Vallon, 1993), 359.

8. Dormont, "Les dépenses de santé," 401; my emphasis.

9. The technical term is "marginal cost." Economists speak in this case of the "convexity" of the cost curve.

10. On this interpretation, the value of a human life is treated as an index rather than as a magnitude. In the case of a magnitude—a quantity of heat, say—it is meaningful to say that this quantity is twice, or perhaps a third, of another such quantity; in the case of an index—a temperature, for example—the most one can say is that a given value is less than, equal to, or greater than another. Thus, for example, relative proportions are not preserved in moving from one method of calculating an index value to another, say, from degrees Fahrenheit to degrees Celsius. But some economists, not content with treating the value of human life as an index, have sought to raise it to the status of a magnitude. In the work of Gary Becker and others, the measure generally applied is a person's willingness to pay: tell me what you are prepared to pay to have your life prolonged by a year and I will tell you what it is worth. In its most demented form, this kind of economism holds that the value of a person's life is to be calculated as a function of the value of the market goods and services he is capable of producing.

    Thus, for example, the Intergovernmental Panel on Climate Change (IPCC) undertook in one of its first reports to assign a monetary value to the expected global impact of climate change. This meant putting damage to the Gulf and Atlantic coastlines of the United States caused by the increased frequency and violence of hurricanes on the same level with the disappearance of a large part of Bangladesh as a result of rising sea levels. In order to compare human losses in the two cases, estimates were made on the basis of per capita GDP—with the morally absurd result that the life of an American was reckoned to be worth one hundred times more than the life of a Bangladeshi. Faced with the threat of resignation by the representatives of the world's poorest countries, the IPCC sheepishly put away its calculations in a drawer, where, thankfully, they remain still today. It cannot be emphasized forcefully enough that philosophy—the analysis of concepts—serves a noble purpose when it helps to derail the maddest schemes of economistic technocrats.

11. Friedrich Nietzsche, *Twilight of the Idols, or, How to Philosophize with a Hammer*, ed. and trans. Duncan Large (Oxford: Oxford University Press, 1998), 61. Emphasis in the original.

12. I use this term in the sense given it by Adolphe Quetelet (1796–1874), the founder of what used to be called "moral statistics."

13. I myself have had the opportunity to study at first hand an extreme case of the statistical dissolution of personal identity, in which a *zero* value was placed on human life: the aftermath of the nuclear accident at Chernobyl. Never has a historical event given rise to such contrary findings. Setting the official figure of a few dozen deaths against the one that is given by some observers in the contaminated area, where some ten million people live, in the hundreds of thousands, one obtains a ratio of roughly 1 to 10,000. This colossal divergence cannot be satisfactorily explained by blaming the dishonesty of some and the resentment of others. At bottom, the issue is philosophical in character, and raises two questions of principle. In the first place, some actions have an extremely small probability of producing a considerable effect. Because they are statistically insignificant, ought a moral calculus hold these probabilities to be null? Second, some actions having imperceptible consequences nevertheless affect a very large number of persons. Because they are imperceptible, can these consequences legitimately be assumed not to exist? In the case of Chernobyl, since the radioactive exposure was spread out in time and

distributed over a vast population, it is impossible to assert with confidence that a person who dies from cancer or leukemia has died as a result of the accident there. The most one can say is that the prior probability of dying from cancer or leukemia was very slightly increased as a result of the accident. The tens of thousands of deaths that may reasonably be assumed, in my view, to have been caused by the accident therefore cannot be *named*. The official position is to conclude from this that they did not occur. See my *Retour de Tchernobyl: Journal d'un homme en colère* (Paris: Seuil, 2006).

14. Jean de la Fontaine, *The Complete Fables*, trans. Norman R. Shapiro (Urbana: University of Illinois Press, 2007), 8.1, 188.

15. Jean de La Bruyère, *Les Caractères, ou, Les mœurs de ce siècle*, 11.38 (Paris: H. Didier, 1933), 398.

16. Strictly speaking, one should refer to the *expected value* of the number of years left to live. In what follows I use the word "average" solely in this probabilistic sense.

17. Probability theorists call it a normal (or Gaussian) distribution.

18. Pólya's urn experiment, described in the previous chapter, illustrates this phenomenon.

19. See the Report of the Commission on the Measurement of Economic Performance and Social Progress, 14 September 2009; available online at http://www.stiglitz-sen-fitoussi.fr/en/index.htm.

20. Mandelbrot published this parable for the first time in "Forecasts of Future Prices, Unbiased Markets, and Martingale Models," *Journal of Business* 39 (January 1966): 242–55. Modified versions later appeared in both French and English: see, for example, "Hasards et tourbillons: Quatre contes à clefs," *Les Annales des Mines* (November 1975): 61–66 (available online at http://math.yale.edu/mandelbrot/web_pdfs/078hasardsettourbillons.pdf); and Benoît B. Mandelbrot and Richard L. Hudson, *The (Mis)Behavior of Markets: A Fractal View of Risk, Ruin, and Reward* (New York: Basic Books, 2004), 242–43. This premonitory book, which foresaw the crisis of 2007–8 several years in advance, seems to have gone almost entirely unnoticed. And yet, as Mandelbrot remarked in an interview that appeared shortly before his death ("Il était inévitable que des choses très graves se produisent," *Le Monde* [18–19 October 2009]), it was inevitable that a very serious crisis would occur. See also Mandelbrot, *Fractals and Scaling in Finance: Discontinuity, Concentration, Risk* (New York: Springer, 1997).

21. See Günther Anders, *Die Antiquiertheit des Menschen: Über die Seele im Zeitalter der zweiten industriellen Revolution* (Munich: Beck, 1956); also *Hiroshima ist überall* (Munich: Beck, 1982). [Both these works have been translated into French, though not into English; see, in the latter case, chapter 1, n. 7 above.—Trans.]

22. See Mandelbrot's 1966 article on Martingale models, cited in n. 20 above; also Dupuy, *La panique*, 102–4.

23. Christian Walter and Michel de Pracontal, in *Le virus B*, show that the world of finance remains incurably attached to the bell curve, or law of normal distribution (the "B" of the book's title refers to Brownian motion, a random walk whose steps are governed by this law). The authors attribute a large part of the recent financial crisis to the chronic and flagrant underestimation of the likelihood of extreme events, which they see as the result less of perverse institutional incentives than of a culpable unwillingness to see the world as it really is. Nassim Nicholas Taleb's best seller, *The Black Swan: The Impact of the Highly Improbable*, 2nd ed. (New York: Random House, 2010), deals less satisfactorily with the same topic.

24. See Jean-Pierre Dupuy, *Pour un catastrophisme éclairé: Quand l'impossible est certain* (Paris: Seuil, 2002), 175–97.

25. Known variously as the Paradox of the Unexpected Hanging, the Hangman Paradox, and the Prediction Paradox. W. V. O. Quine published a particularly subtle commentary sixty years ago, "On a So-Called Paradox," *Mind* 62 (1953): 65–66.

26. In mathematical terms one would say that the *state* of the system at any given moment depends on assuming that the *derivative* of the state vector will go on being positive indefinitely.

27. See Peter A. Thiel, "The Optimistic Thought Experiment," *Policy Review*, no. 147 (29 January 2008); available online at http://www.hoover.org/publications/policy-review/article/5646. (My research in this field has been partly sponsored by Imitatio, a project of the Thiel Foundation.)

28. See Dupuy, *The Mark of the Sacred*, 1–19.

Chapter 4. Critique of Economic Reason

1. See, for example, Annette Disselkamp's book *L'éthique protestante de Max Weber* (Paris: Presses Universitaires de France, 1994), a revised version of her Sorbonne doctoral dissertation supervised by Raymond Boudon. Disselkamp's book is remarkable for two reasons: first, because it presents in a clear and comprehensive manner the main issues of the controversy aroused by Weber's work ever since its publication almost a century ago; second, because in reproaching Weber for having sought to explain the formation of the spirit of capitalism in exclusively religious terms, without taking into account the actual course of social history, it is led astray by a failure to grasp the logical structure of what I call projected time.

2. Pierre Chaunu, *Église, culture et société: Essais sur Réforme et Contre-Réforme, 1517–1620* (Paris: Société d'édition d'enseignement supérieur, 1981), 46.

3. The German word used by Weber, *Beruf*, has the dual sense of a profession and a calling. Talcott Parsons, whose much-criticized 1930 translation was long the standard edition of Weber's work in English, used both these terms in alternation while avoiding "vocation," which seemed to him not to carry the ethical connotation intended by Weber; see *The Protestant Ethic and the Spirit of Capitalism* (New York: Scribner's, 1958), 194 n. 11. Weber's most recent translator, Stephen Kalberg, sees the matter differently, using either "vocation" or "vocational calling." For Weber, he says, the term denotes a task given by God; see *The Protestant Ethic and the Spirit of Capitalism* (New York: Oxford University Press, 2010), 30–31, 426.—Trans.

4. Weber, *The Protestant Ethic and the Spirit of Capitalism*, 1.2.5, trans. Kalberg, 161; see also 170.

5. See ibid., 1.2.4, 337 n. 76.

6. Ibid., 124.

7. Ibid., 125.

8. Ibid.

9. Ibid., 128.

10. Ibid., 120. Emphasis in the original.

11. Ibid., 1.2.5, 172; 1.2.5, 370 n. 8, 372 n. 15. Emphasis in the original.

12. Ibid., 1.2.4, 337–38 n. 76. Emphasis in the original. [The Latin has been interpreted in a way that is closer to the wording in Parsons's version, which here, and in other places as well, is still to be preferred in my view to Kalberg's new translation. On the history and difficulties of translating Weber, see W. G. Runciman's penetrating review of the new edition of the methodological

writings edited by Hans Henrik Braun and Sam Whimster (New York: Routledge, 2012), "The English Weber," *Times Literary Supplement* (28 September 2012), 7–8.—Trans.]

13. See ibid., 124.

14. Disselkamp, *L'éthique protestante de Max Weber*, 124.

15. N. H. Keeble, *Richard Baxter, Puritan Man of Letters* (Oxford: Clarendon Press, 1982), 69. My emphasis.

16. On the view held by Puritan preachers of their duty as "physicians of the soul," and the related doctrine of salvation by virtue of grace and faith alone, see William Haller, *The Rise of Puritanism, or, The Way to the New Jerusalem as Set Forth in Pulpit and Press from Thomas Cartwright to John Lilburne and John Milton, 1570–1643* (New York: Columbia University Press, 1938), especially 86–91.

17. See Alain Peyrefitte, *La société de confiance: Essais sur les origines et la nature du développement* (Paris: Odile Jacob, 1995), 199–121. *"No to fatalism*: the whole of Dutch behavior expresses this refusal," Peyrefitte notes. "And yet this republic was Calvinist; it was founded on the energy concentrated in men prepared to die on behalf of the idea of predestination. *There is something paradoxical about this"* (119; my emphasis). The paradox vanishes at once if one adopts a compatibilist perspective. See also Peyrefitte's Collège de France lectures, *Du "miracle" en économie* (Paris: Odile Jacob, 1995).

18. Disselkamp, *L'éthique protestante de Max Weber*, 138.

19. William Perkins, *A Case of Conscience: The Greatest that Euer Was; How a Man May Knowe Whether He Be a Child of God or No* (1592), reprinted in *The Workes of that Famous and Worthy Minister of Christ in the University of Cambridge, Mr. William Perkins*, 3 vols. (London: J. Legatt, 1613–1616), 1:435, 437; quoted in Disselkamp, *L'éthique protestante de Max Weber*, 138–39. The emphasis is mine.

20. Ibid., 140. My emphasis.

21. Perkins, in *Workes*, 1:438; quoted in ibid., 139.

22. Ibid. The emphasis is mine.

23. Nor should Weber be reproached for having failed to unravel them: the analytical techniques that make this possible were only developed in the last quarter of the twentieth century, long after his death. Latter-day commentators cannot claim the same excuse.

24. Disselkamp, *L'éthique protestante de Max Weber*, 101.

25. This axiom is expressed in terms of preferences: if a subject prefers an option p to another option q, where the state of the world belongs to a subset X; and if he also prefers p to q in the complement of X, then, if he is rational, he prefers p to q even if he does not know whether the state of the world belongs to X or to its complement.

26. Pierre Choderlos de Laclos, *Les liaisons dangereuses,* ed. and trans. Douglas Parmée (Oxford: Oxford University Press, 1995), Letter 152, 335. The emphasis and bracketed gloss are mine.

27. See ibid., Letter 153, 336–37.

28. The argument that Merteuil presses upon Valmont beautifully illustrates this sophism—much more so, in fact, than it exemplifies the argument from strategic dominance. It is clear that Valmont's attitude has an impact on Merteuil's decision whether or not to cheat on him. If Merteuil is no less jealous of Valmont than Valmont is of her, then Valmont can hope to dominate

Merteuil only by being an unfaithful lover in his turn. The case in which he remains faithful to Merteuil and wins her heart is thereby excluded, and the argument from strategic dominance collapses of its own weight.

29. I am among those who suspect that William Newcomb never existed; or rather, that William Newcomb is a pseudonym of the late social and political philosopher Robert Nozick, who was the first person to write about this paradox, attributing it to a fictive source—while identifying Newcomb as a physicist working at Livermore Radiation Laboratory (as Lawrence Livermore was then known) in California. Nozick's own early work, as a student of the philosopher of science Carl Gustav Hempel at Princeton, was on the philosophy of quantum mechanics. His statement of the paradox is found in "Newcomb's Problem and Two Principles of Choice," in *Essays in Honor of Carl G. Hempel: A Tribute on the Occasion of His Sixty-Fifth Birthday*, ed. Nicholas Rescher (Dordrecht: D. Reidel, 1970), 114–15.

30. Notably Amos Tversky, who performed this test on his students at Stanford. See n. 39 below.

31. This proposition is technically known as a common-cause Newcomb problem. Max Weber's problem comes under the same head. A single cause, in this case a divine decree, is responsible both for my election and for the fact that I behave as though I were one of the elect. If I did not behave as one of the elect, it would have been because the divine decree did not favor me and I was damned.

32. In Bergson's metaphysics it is possibility that behaves in this manner. See Henri Bergson, "The Possible and the Real," in *The Creative Mind: An Introduction to Metaphysics,* trans. Mabelle L. Andison (New York: Philosophical Library, 1946), 119–21; also my discussion in *The Mark of the Sacred*, 201–2.

33. In this connection see the work of the cultural anthropologist George M. Foster, notably *Traditional Societies and Technological Change*, 2nd ed. (New York: Harper and Row, 1973).

34. A rigorous demonstration of these propositions within the framework of metaphysical logic may be found in the appendix.

35. One of the most effective ways to bring out the differences between the two major approaches to the philosophy of mind, embodied by the analytic and Continental traditions, is to compare the treatment of these twin themes in the work of Davidson and Sartre, as I myself have discovered from my teaching over the years at Stanford.

36. See Donald Davidson, "Deception and Division," in *The Multiple Self*, ed. Jon Elster (Cambridge: Cambridge University Press, 1986), 79–92.

37. See Donald Davidson, "Two Paradoxes of Irrationality," in *Philosophical Essays on Freud*, ed. Richard Wollheim and James Hopkins (Cambridge: Cambridge University Press, 1982), 289–305.

38. Weber, *The Protestant Ethic and the Spirit of Capitalism*, 1.2.4, trans. Kalberg, 125. The French translation of this phrase ("saints débordant de confiance en soi") is stronger, and, I believe, more faithful to Weber's meaning here. They are not merely self-confident, but overflowing with confidence—supremely self-confident. Some commentators even speak of "self-proclaimed saints."

39. See Eldar Shafir and Amos Tversky, "Thinking through Uncertainty: Nonconsequential Reasoning and Choice," *Cognitive Psychology* 24, no. 4 (1992): 449–74.

40. Jean-Paul Sartre, *L'être et le néant: Essai d'ontologie phénoménologique* (Gallimard, 2006), 4.1.2B, 554. The emphasis is mine. [The deeply flawed English version by Hazel E. Barnes has remained

uncorrected since its publication in 1956, without being superseded by a fresh translation. My own renderings, approved by the author, are given here and below.—Trans.]

41. Ibid., 4.1.3, 614. Emphasis in the original.

42. Thus Renaut's rendering of the German term in his book on Sartre by the hyphenated expression *réalité-humaine*. Elsewhere he translates *Dasein* simply as "human being"; see, for example, Renaut, *The Era of the Individual,* 178.—Trans.

43. Alain Renaut, *Sartre, le dernier philosophe* (Paris: Grasset, 1993), 49. Emphasis in the original.

44. Ibid., 48.

45. Sartre, *L'être et le néant*, 4.1.2E, 604. My emphasis.

46. Ibid., 4.1.1, 523. Emphasis in the original.

47. Ibid., 524. Emphasis in the original.

48. Ibid., 1.2.2, 90–91.

49. Ibid., 104.

50. Ibid.

51. Ibid., 1.2.3, 106.

52. Ibid.

53. Ibid.

54. See Renaut, *Sartre*, 180.

55. Sartre, *L'être et le néant*, 1.2.3, 104.

56. Ibid. Recall that, on Sartre's view, for bad faith to be possible, sincerity itself must be bad faith (note 49 above).

57. Ibid., 105. Emphasis in the original.

58. Ibid. Emphasis in the original.

59. Ibid. Emphasis in the original.

60. Ibid., 1.2.1, 84.

61. Jean-Paul Sartre, "Explication de *L'Étranger*" (February 1943), reprinted in Sartre, *Situations I,* rev. and aug. ed. (Paris: Gallimard, 2010), 142. The emphasis is mine. [Here and below I have made my own translations, in preference to the ones found in Annette Michelson's 1955 English version of Sartre's essay.—Trans.]

62. Ibid.

63. See René Girard, "Camus's Stranger Retried," *PMLA* 79 (December 1964): 519–33; reprinted in Girard, *"To Double Business Bound": Essays on Literature, Mimesis, and Anthropology* (Baltimore: Johns Hopkins University Press, 1978), 9–35.

64. Ibid., 14. The emphasis in the first instance is mine.

65. Sartre, *L'être et le néant*, 1.2.2, 91. Emphasis in the original.

66. Sartre, "Explication de *L'Étranger*," in *Situations I*, 136. The emphasis is mine.

67. Thus the title of Sartre's famous 1946 lecture, "L'existentialisme est un humanisme." See Renaut, *Sartre*, 203.

68. Heidegger coined the term *mit-sein* to signify an irreducible dimension of human being, the condition of living with others. Sartre—a prisoner of his own solipsistic conception of bad faith, equaled only by the solipsism of Davidson's notion of self-deception—refers to the idea, but makes no use of it.

69. Smith, *The Theory of Moral Sentiments*, 3.2, 150.

70. See ibid., 152–54. In this connection Smith contrasts poets, who are especially vulnerable to the unfavorable judgments of the crowd and, for this reason, quick to "form themselves into factions and cabals" and to enter into "intrigue in order to secure the public applause," with mathematicians and natural philosophers, who tend to have "the most perfect assurance" and who are "frequently very indifferent about the reception which they may meet with from the public" (148–49). How true this is still today—though today, it must be said, some scientists and mathematicians behave no better than poets!

71. See ibid., 147–55.

72. I refer here to the second chapter of Part III ("Of the love of Praise, and of that of Praise-worthiness; and of the dread of Blame, and of that of Blameworthiness"), from which all of the preceding quotations are taken.

73. André Orléan, in his recent book *The Empire of Value*, which I have already cited, has undertaken to thoroughly rethink the concept of economic value. Both the classical tradition, which associates the value of a commodity with the quantity of labor needed to produce it, and the neoclassical tradition, which relates value to utility, treat value as an "objective" magnitude in the sense that its determining factors are situated in the present or the past. In the reconstruction proposed by Orléan, by contrast, value is considered to be a trace of the *future*, which is to say the reflection in the present of a path that has yet to be traveled. The uncertainty of economic life has the consequence that several prices for any commodity are possible, because several futures are possible. Accordingly, there is nothing in the least neutral about valuation. It is never a measure of what is, but always the expression of a point of view in the service of someone's interest. It is an act by which society decides which paths will be followed and which ones will be left unexplored.

Conclusion. The Way Out from Fatalism

1. The demonstration of this last point is rather involved. See the appendix following.

2. I refer the reader to two of my earlier works, both previously cited, in which this dual paradox is discussed at length: *Pour un catastrophisme éclairé*, 151–216; and *Petite métaphysique des tsunamis*, 91–107.

Appendix. Time, Paradox

1. By definition, p materially implies q if and only if either p is false or q is true.

2. See Alvin Plantinga, "On Ockham's Way Out," *Faith and Philosophy* 3 (1986): 235–69.

3. See Jean-Pierre Dupuy, "Two Temporalities, Two Rationalities: A New Look at Newcomb's Paradox," in *Economics and Cognitive Science*, ed. Paul Bourgine and Bernard Walliser (New York: Pergamon, 1992), 191–220.

4. See Jean-Pierre Dupuy, "Temps et rationalité: Les paradoxes du raisonnement rétrograde," in *Les limites de la rationalité*, 2 vols., ed. Jean-Pierre Dupuy and Pierre Livet (Paris: La Découverte, 1997), 1:30–58; and "Rationality and Self-Deception," in *Self-Deception and Paradoxes of Rationality*, ed. Jean-Pierre Dupuy (Stanford: CSLI Publications, 1998), 113–50.

5. Very few rational choice theorists would agree that an assurance game in this simple form constitutes an example of a backward induction paradox. Much more complicated versions, such as the Centipede game, are needed before they will recognize the existence of such a difficulty. One of the advantages of my theory is that its paradigmatic application is the assurance game, the logic of which has universal relevance. See Jean-Pierre Dupuy, "Philosophical Foundations of a New Concept of Equilibrium in the Social Sciences: Projected Equilibrium," *Philosophical Studies* 100 (2000): 323–45.

6. "Our submarines are capable of killing fifty million people in a half hour," a French nuclear strategist warned some twenty-five years ago. "We think that this suffices to deter any adversary."

7. The discontinuity encountered at $\varepsilon = 0$ suggests that a sort of indeterminacy principle is at work here. The weights ε and $1 - \varepsilon$ behave like probabilities in quantum mechanics, so that the fixed point must be conceived in projected time as the *superposition* of two states, one the accidental *and* inevitable occurrence of catastrophe, the other its nonoccurrence.

8. "Wo aber Gefahr ist, wächst / das Rettende auch." Friedrich Hölderlin, *Patmos* (1808), in *Sämtliche Werke und Briefe*, 3 vols., ed. Jochen Schmidt (Frankfurt am Main: Deutscher Klassiker Verlag, 1992), 1:350.

Index